THE UNCANNY X-MEN

LEGACY OF THE LOST

CHRIS CLAREMONT • JOHN ROMITA JR.
DAN GREEN • BARRY WINDSOR SMITH

MARVEL POCKET BOOK The Uncanny X-Men: Legacy Of The Lost

The Uncanny X-Men: Legacy Of The Lost. Marvel Pocketbook Vol. 13. Contains material originally published in magazine form as X-Men #185-191. First printing 2011. Published by Panini Publishing, a division of Panini UK Limited. Mike Riddell, Managing Director. Alan O'Keefe, Managing Editor. Mark Irvine, Production Manager. Marco M. Lupoi, Publishing Director Europe. Ed Hammond, Reprint Editor. Charlotte Reilly, Designer. Office of publication: Brockbourne House, 77 Mount Ephraim, Tunbridge Wells, Kent TN4 8BS. MARVEL, X-Men and all related characters and the distinctive likenesses thereof: TM & © 1984, 1985 & 2011 Marvel Entertainment, LLC and its subsidiaries. Licensed by Marvel Characters B.V. No similarity between any of the names, characters, persons and/or institutions in this edition with those of any living or dead person or institution is intended, and any such similarity which may exist is purely coincidental. This publication may not be sold, except by authorised dealers, and is sold subject to the condition that it shall not be sold or distributed with any part of its cover or markings removed, nor in a mutilated condition. This publication is produced under licence from Marvel Characters B.V. through Panini S.p.A. Printed in the U.K. www.marvel.com. All rights reserved. ISBN: 978-1-84653-138-5

THE UNCANNY X-MEN
LEGACY OF THE LOST

CONTENTS

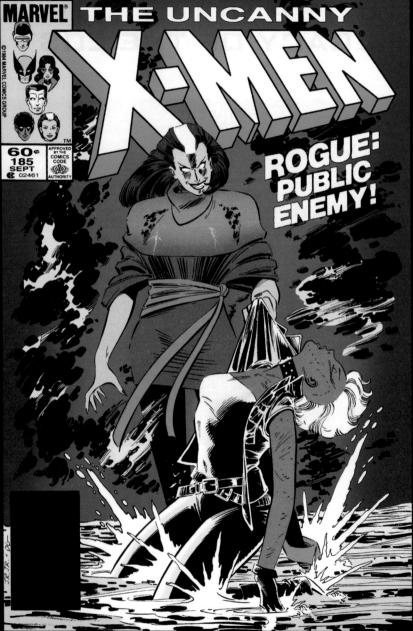

SOME MONTHS AGO, SHE WAS INVOLVED IN A BATTLE ON THESE VERY PREMISES WITH A TEAM OF SO-CALLED SUPER HEROES-- ALSO MUTANTS-- THE *X-MEN.*

THESE FILMS-- TAKEN AT THE TIME-- ILLUSTRATE HER VARIOUS ABILITIES: PHENOMENAL STRENGTH, INVULNERABILITY...

... AND, DEADLIEST OF ALL, THE POWER TO ABSORB THE THOUGHTS, MEMORIES, AND PHYSICAL TALENTS OF WHOMEVER SHE TOUCHES-- IN THIS CASE, THE X-MEN'S LEADER, *STORM.*

THIS TRANSFERAL CAN BE TEMPORARY OR PERMANENT, DEPENDING ON LENGTH OF CONTACT.

THOUGH ORIGINALLY AFFILIATED WITH THE *BROTHERHOOD OF EVIL MUTANTS,* ROGUE HAS OF LATE BEEN OPERATING WITH THE X-MEN. IN ALL PROBABILITY, THEREFORE, SHE WAS NOT FIGHTING THEM IN EARNEST, BUT MERELY PROVIDING A DIVERSION, ALLOWING ANOTHER TEAMMATE TO PENETRATE OUR PRIME DATA BANK AND ERASE ALL REFERENCES TO THE X-MEN-- AND MUTANTS IN GENERAL-- FROM THE ENTIRE FEDERAL COMPUTER NETWORK.

A FURTHER POSSIBILITY IS THAT THE X-MEN AND BROTHERHOOD HAVE FORMED AN ALLIANCE-- THEY MAY EVEN HAVE BEEN WORKING SECRETLY TOGETHER FROM THE OUTSET.

FINALLY, ROGUE RECENTLY EFFECTED THE ESCAPE OF AN AS YET UNIDENTIFIED OPERATIVE FROM *SHIELD* CUSTODY. DURING THIS ACTION, SHE KILLED ONE OF COLONEL FURY'S AGENTS.

OUR ASSIGNMENT IS TO BRING HER TO JUSTICE.

THIS WEAPON, PROVIDED BY THE ARMORER *FORGE,* IS DESIGNED TO NEUTRALIZE THE SUPER-POWERS OF ITS TARGETS.

ONE GOOD SHOT WILL, ESSENTIALLY, TRANSFORM ROGUE INTO A NORMAL HUMAN BEING.

2

GYRICH!!

THIS IS A PRIVATE BRIEFING, DR. DARKHÖLME. YOU HAVE NO BUSINESS HERE.

I'LL BE MORE THAN HAPPY TO LEAVE...

...ONCE I HAVE FORGE'S NEUTRALIZER!

RAVEN, CALM DOWN!

THE BLAZES I WILL! THAT PROJECT'S TOP SECRET! GYRICH SHOULDN'T EVEN KNOW OF THE GUN'S EXISTENCE...

...MUCH LESS POSSESS THE ONLY FUNCTIONAL PROTOTYPE!

I HAVE AUTHORIZATION, DOCTOR.

IT'S UNTESTED, YOU FOOL! WE'VE NO IDEA WHAT EFFECT IT'LL HAVE--!

THEN THIS WOULD SEEM AN IDEAL OPPORTUNITY TO LEARN.

WHAT--?! VAL-- THIS WAS *YOUR* IDEA--?!!

I'M SORRY, RAVEN. I UNDERSTAND YOUR FEELINGS-- BUT ROGUE'S A KILLER, AND THIS WEAPON MAY BE THE ONLY MEANS OF SAFELY DEALING WITH HER.

IF IT DOESN'T WORK, WE'RE NO WORSE OFF THAN BEFORE.

BUT IF IT DOES-- THINK OF THE RAMIFICATIONS! WE'D NO LONGER HAVE TO LIVE IN TERROR OF SUPER-VILLAINS. ONE ZAP, AND THEIR POWERS ARE GONE, THE THREAT REMOVED.

I'LL PROTEST--!

WASTE OF TIME. THIS POLICY DECISION CAME FROM THE OVAL OFFICE.

LIKE IT OR NOT, RAVEN, YOU'LL JUST HAVE TO LIVE WITH IT.

3

PROFESSOR CHARLES XAVIER'S SCHOOL FOR GIFTED YOUNGSTERS -- SALEM CENTER, NEW YORK...

PROFESSOR! FORGIVE MY INTERRUPTION-- BUT ROGUE IS GONE!

ARE YOU CERTAIN, STORM--WHEN DID THIS HAPPEN?!

SOMETIME LAST NIGHT.

HER BED HAS NOT BEEN SLEPT IN AND THE CLOSET IS EMPTY. SHE LEFT NO NOTE.

EXCUSE US A MOMENT, RACHEL.

SURE, PROFESSOR-- I UNDERSTAND.

WE'LL CONTINUE OUR SESSION UPON MY RETURN.

I CAN'T SENSE ROGUE'S THOUGHTS. THAT PLACES HER BEYOND THE NEW YORK METROPOLITAN AREA.

YOUR CONCERN-- AND DISTRESS-- ARE OBVIOUS, ORORO. WHY?

THESE PAST WEEKS-- EVER SINCE HER ENCOUNTER WITH *MICHAEL ROSSI*-- ROGUE HAS BECOME INCREASINGLY TENSE AND UNSTABLE...

...REBUFFING ALL MY ATTEMPTS TO HELP.

*X-MEN #182 --ANN.

EVIDENTLY, SHE MANAGED TO HIDE HER CONDITION FROM YOU...

...AND SINCE ROSSI IS AWAY ON A MISSION, I HAVE BEEN UNABLE TO GET HIS EXPLANATION.

ROGUE TURNED TO THE X-MEN BECAUSE HER POWERS WERE DRIVING HER INSANE.

WE THOUGHT SHE WAS GETTING BETTER.

BUT NOW, I AM DESPERATELY AFRAID SHE MAY BE SUFFERING A RELAPSE!

FOLLOW ME TO MY LAB. WE'LL USE MY CEREBRO PSI- SCANNER TO TRY TO FIND HER.

4

ROGUE WAS ONE OF THE X-MEN WHO RESCUED ME FROM SELENE*, BUT I DON'T REMEMBER HER.

SO WHAT ELSE IS NEW? THE MORE I SEE OF THIS ERA, THE LESS MY MEMORIES MEAN ANYTHING.

*LAST ISH-- ANN.

I HURLED MYSELF BACK IN TIME TO SAVE MY FUTURE EARTH FROM DESTRUCTION.

I NEVER DREAMED I'D END UP IN THE WRONG PAST.

I WONDER HOW DEEP THE DIFFERENCES RUN?

THERE'S AN ENTRY FOR CYCLOPS--

-- BUT IT'S IN ALASKA! WHAT'S HE DOING THERE?!

I'M MAKING A MISTAKE-- I SHOULDN'T CALL-- BUT TO HEAR HIS VOICE AGAIN, TO KNOW HE'S ALIVE AND THAT SOME THINGS CAN'T CHANGE, NO MATTER WHAT--!

HELLO?

HELLO-- THIS IS SCOTT SUMMERS, IS ANYONE THERE?!

WHAT'S UP, HON?

NO ANSWER-- PROBABLY A CRANK...

...OR A WRONG NUMBER.

DADDY!

MOM!

5

THE PENTAGON.

ACCESS TO THIS SUB-LEVEL OF THE SPRAWLING COMPLEX IS RESTRICTED BY RAVEN DARKHÖLME TO A VERY SELECT FEW.

NONE WORK FOR THE GOVERNMENT. THEIR LOYALTY IS TO HER.

THEY COMPRISE THE BROTHERHOOD OF EVIL MUTANTS, AND RAVEN--IN HER GUISE AS THE SHAPE-CHANGER, MYSTIQUE--IS THEIR LEADER.

THESE SECRET, HIDDEN CHAMBERS ARE THE GROUP'S OPERATIONAL HEADQUARTERS.

IRENÉ!

I WASN'T EXPECTING YOU, BUT I'M GLAD YOU'RE HERE. IT HAS BEEN A BRUTAL DAY.

ROGUE IS IN GRAVE DANGER.

I KNOW.

VAL COOPER AND HENRY GYRICH WANT TO MAKE AN EXAMPLE OF HER, TO PROVE THE GOVERNMENT CAN HANDLE SUPER-CRIMINALS WITHOUT THE AID OF HEROES LIKE THE AVENGERS. FORGE'S NEUTRAL-IZER MAY GIVE THEM THE MEANS TO DO IT.

WHAT ARE YOUR INTENTIONS, RAVEN?

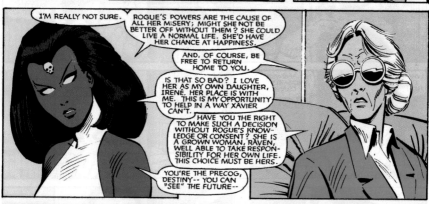

I'M REALLY NOT SURE. ROGUE'S POWERS ARE THE CAUSE OF ALL HER MISERY; MIGHT SHE NOT BE BETTER OFF WITHOUT THEM? SHE COULD LIVE A NORMAL LIFE. SHE'D HAVE HER CHANCE AT HAPPINESS.

AND, OF COURSE, BE FREE TO RETURN HOME TO YOU.

IS THAT SO BAD? I LOVE HER AS MY OWN DAUGHTER, IRENÉ. HER PLACE IS WITH ME. THIS IS MY OPPORTUNITY TO HELP IN A WAY XAVIER CAN'T.

HAVE YOU THE RIGHT TO MAKE SUCH A DECISION WITHOUT ROGUE'S KNOW-LEDGE OR CONSENT? SHE IS A GROWN WOMAN, RAVEN, WELL ABLE TO TAKE RESPON-SIBILITY FOR HER OWN LIFE. THIS CHOICE MUST BE HERS.

YOU'RE THE PRECOG, DESTINY-- YOU CAN "SEE" THE FUTURE--

-- TELL ME WHICH COURSE OF ACTION IS BEST FOR ROGUE.

I WISH I COULD. BUT THESE PAST FEW DAYS, MY PERCEPTIONS HAVE BECOME JUMBLED--

-- AS IF THE VERY FABRIC OF TIME ITSELF HAS BEEN RENT ASUNDER.

I AM SORRY, RAVEN. THE ONLY ADVICE I CAN OFFER...

... IS THAT YOU FOLLOW THE DICTATES OF YOUR HEART.

6

A MILITARY TRANSPORT, OUTBOUND FROM WASHINGTON'S ANDREWS AIR FORCE BASE...

ORDINARILY, HENRY, THIS SORT OF MISSION WOULD BE HANDLED BY *SHIELD*.* BUT THEY'RE THE SPEARHEAD OF OUR WAR WITH THE DIRE WRAITHS;** THEY SIMPLY HAVEN'T THE RESOURCES TO SPARE.

* *SUPREME HEADQUARTERS INTELLIGENCE, ESPIONAGE, LAW-ENFORCEMENT DIVISION;*

** FOR DETAILS, SEE CURRENT ISSUES OF ROM --ME AGAIN.

MY PEOPLE ARE THE BEST THE FBI AND SECRET SERVICE HAVE TO OFFER, DR. COOPER. WE WON'T DISAPPOINT YOU.

HOW WILL YOU LOCATE ROGUE WITH FORGE'S SCANNER?

NO-- ITS RANGE IS TOO LIMITED. THIS MODULE IS WHAT THE AVENGERS USED TO TRACK HER WHEN THEY FOUGHT A WHILE AGO.* THE GIRL'S PHYSIOLOGY IS A SYNTHESIS OF HUMAN AND ALIEN.

*AVENGERS ANNUAL #10-- GUESS WHO?

HER HYBRID METABOLISM GENERATES A UNIQUE ENERGY AURA; THIS PICKS IT UP. WE'VE ALREADY GOT A GENERAL FIX ON HER POSITION. THE CLOSER WE COME, THE MORE WE'LL REFINE THE CONTACT, UNTIL WE'VE GOT HER NAILED.

I WANT HER ALIVE, HENRY.

WE'LL DO OUR BEST, MA'AM-- BUT NO GUARANTEES.

DALLAS, TEXAS.

SHE'S DONE WHAT!?!

OUR AGREEMENT-- FROM THE BEGINNING, RAVEN-- WAS THAT MY WEAPONS WERE NOT TO BE USED, UNDER *ANY* CIRCUMSTANCES, UNTIL I RELEASED THEM!

WHAT CAN I SAY, FORGE-- VAL CHANGED THE RULES.

I PROTESTED-- I SCREAMED BLOODY MURDER-- AND WAS TOLD, IN EFFECT, TO MIND MY OWN BUSINESS.

DOESN'T SHE REALIZE IT'S UNTESTED?!

THE IMPRESSION I RECEIVED IS THAT SHE DOESN'T MUCH CARE.

HER ONLY CONCERN IS CAPTURING ROGUE.

7

RAVEN, I'VE NO IDEA WHETHER THE GUN REMOVES POWERS TEMPORARILY OR PERMANENTLY-- OR WHAT MIGHT HAPPEN TO THE PERSON IN THE PROCESS. IT COULD CAUSE INCALCULABLE DAMAGE--

--IT MIGHT EVEN KILL!

THAT'S WHY I PHONED, FORGE. NO ONE IN AUTHORITY'LL LISTEN TO ME.

I'M HOPING-- PRAYING--YOU HAVE BETTER LUCK.

IF I DON'T, RAY...

...THE GOVERNMENT CAN FIND ITSELF ANOTHER INVENTOR.

THIS IS FORGE--

--I WANT TO SPEAK TO THE PRESIDENT!

CALDECOTT COUNTY, ON THE BANKS OF THE MISSISSIPPI...

THIS IS FARMING COUNTRY, WHERE ONCE COTTON WAS KING AND STATELY MANSIONS LINED THE RIVER, SETTING A STANDARD FOR STYLE AND AFFLUENT, GRACIOUS LIVING THAT WAS THE ENVY OF THE WORLD. IT WAS A WAY OF LIFE PEOPLE BELIEVED WOULD LAST FOREVER.

BUT THE KING HAS LONG-SINCE BEEN DETHRONED, AND MOST OF THE GREAT ESTATES FALLEN INTO RUIN.

OF ALL THAT ONCE WAS, ONLY THE RIVER REMAINS.

8

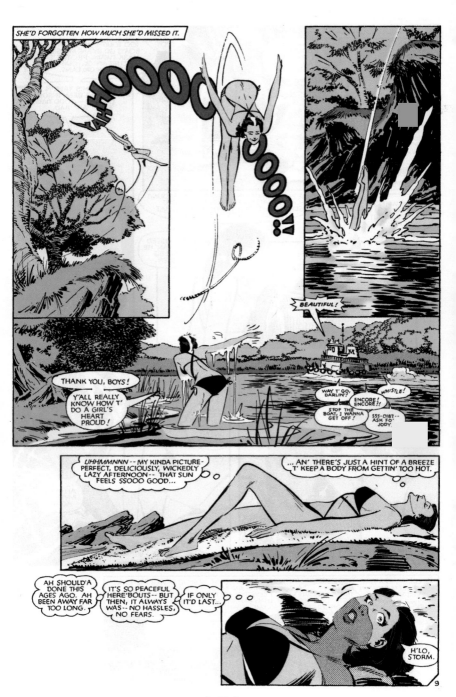

MAY I JOIN YOU, ROGUE?

'S'A FREE COUNTRY-- BUT DON'T COME TOO CLOSE.

AH AIN'T WEARIN' MUCH, AN' ONE TOUCH IS ALL IT'D TAKE T' ZAP YOU.

THIS IS A LOVELY SPOT.

AH'D HIDE OUT HERE, WHEN AH WAS A KID AN' THE WORLD GOT TOO TOUGH. AH'D WATCH THE BOATS GO BY AN' IMAGINE AH WAS MARK TWAIN, PILOTIN' 'EM UP T' NATCHEZ AN' St. LOUIS OR SOUTH T' N'ORLEANS.

THIS TREE'N ME'VE BEEN THROUGH A LOT-- GOOD TIMES, AN' BAD.

HERE'S WHERE AH FIRST LEARNED ABOUT MAH POWER.

ME'N CODY ROBBINS WERE FOOLIN' AROUND-- NECKIN', REALLY-- IT WASN'T ANYTHING SERIOUS, WE JUST WANTED T' SEE WHAT ALL TH' FUSS WAS ABOUT.

AH KISSED HIM-- AN' HE KEELED OVER.

AH THOUGHT AH'D KILLED HIM.

THEN, AH THOUGHT AH WAS GOIN' CRAZY. AH HEARD VOICES IN MY HEAD-- SAW MEM'RIES-- AH KNEW WEREN'T MINE. THEY WERE CODY'S!

AH TRIED T' SHUT 'EM OUT, BUT AH COULDN'T.

SO AH RAN AN' RAN AN' RAN.

AN' AFTER A WHILE, THE VOICES WENT AWAY...

...AN' AH WAS MYSELF AGAIN.

AH GUESS, IN A WAY, AH'VE BEEN RUNNIN' EVER SINCE.

BUT THOSE DAYS ARE PAST. YOU NEED NO LONGER FEAR WHO AND WHAT YOU ARE.

C'MON, ORORO-- AH'VE BEEN AT XAVIER'S SCHOOL FOR MONTHS AN' NOTHIN'S CHANGED. AH STILL CAN'T CONTROL MY POWERS. HECK, AH'M WORSE OFF THAN BEFORE, BECAUSE NOW AH DON'T KNOW ANYMORE WHERE MAH LOYALTIES LIE-- WITH Y'ALL, OR MYSTIQUE!

WE ARE YOUR FRIENDS, ROGUE-- IS THERE NOTHING WE CAN DO?!

10

NO!

REMEMBER WHAT HAPPENED LAST TIME, AT THE PENTAGON?! AH NEARLY TORE THE PLACE APART!

I WAS FIGHTING YOU THEN WITH EVERY OUNCE OF MY BEING. TODAY, I GIVE OF MYSELF FREELY, WITHOUT RESERVATION.

SUPPOSE SOMETHIN' GOES WRONG -- SUPPOSE AH DO T' YOU WHAT AH DID T' CAROL DANVERS -- AN' STEAL YOUR POWERS, YOUR MEM'RIES, YOUR *SELF* -- FOREVER *!*

I AM PREPARED TO TAKE THE RISK.

AH'M AFRAID!

YOU THINK I AM NOT?

ORORO!

GODDESS!

I NEVER IMAGINED THE WORLD COULD BE SO -- *BEAUTIFUL!*

12

THE SUN AND AIR AND WATER-- AH SEE THEM AS PATTERNS OF ENERGY, RESONATING WITHIN MY OWN BEING. AH FEEL... *AWARE* OF EVERY LIVING THING AROUND ME!

MY VOICE IS CHANGING-- *HAH!* -- BECOMING A BLEND OF MINE AND ORORO'S. AH STILL HAVE MAH ACCENT, BUT THE TONE IS DEEPER AND MY SPEECH, MORE FORMAL, LIKE HERS!

THIS IS VERY WEIRD, BUT VERY NEAT!

A WIND HAS SPRUNG UP-- BECAUSE OF MY TRANSFORMATION. CAN AH CALM IT, RETURN THINGS TO THE WAY THEY WERE--?

THERE WE GO-- GENTLY-- THAT DOES THE TRICK!

ORORO CREATES LITTLE RAINSTORMS TO WATER HER PLANTS. AH WONDER IF AH...?

SEEMS EASY ENOUGH-- ALL AH NEED DO IS SHAPE THE APPROPRI- ATE NATURAL FORCES-- CAREFUL, THOUGH-- WITHOUT LETTING THINGS GET OUT OF HAND. THIS IS GREAT -- *OUCH!*

A BOLT OF LIGHTNING FROM THAT CLOUD HIT ME! THE NERVE--!

PLAYTIME IS OVER, GIRL.

BETTER PUT YOUR TOYS AWAY.

PRESTO!

WHATEVER SHALL AH DO FOR AN ENCORE?

13

AH FEEL FULL OF SUCH EXCITEMENT-- AND JOY-- NOTHING SEEMS BEYOND ME! AND BECAUSE ORORO DID NOT RESIST THE TRANSFER...

...HER MEMORIES HAVE YET TO CAUSE ME TROUBLE. PERHAPS THEY NEVER WILL.

AH ONLY WANT A LITTLE MORE, WHAT HARM IS THERE IN THAT?

WHAT AM AH DOING?!

HOW COULD AH EVEN THINK SUCH A THING?! ORORO IS MY FRIEND, IS THIS HOW AH REPAY HER TRUST--

AIUNNGFFF!

FEDERAL OFFICERS, ROGUE!

WE HAVE A WARRANT FOR YOUR ARREST!

WHAT-- STRUCK ME?!

NERVES... TURNED TO... ACID FIRE-- WANT TO CURL UP... DIE -- AN EFFORT... NOT TO SCREAM!

ORORO IS HELPLESS-- WHATEVER... FEDS WANT WITH ME--

-- I CANNOT ABANDON HER.

MUST... DRAW THEM AWAY!

BRIGHT LADY-- I CAN BARELY GET AIRBORNE!

CONCENTRATION... SHOT TO BLAZES-- IMPOSSIBLE TO MAINTAIN... LEVEL FLIGHT. NEVER BEEN SO WEAK-- WHAT DID THEY... DO TO ME?!!

14

TREES -- NO TIME, NO STRENGTH TO CLIMB ABOVE THEM!

OWW!

THE BRANCHES -- HURT!

I SHOULD BE INVULNERABLE -- THAT ENERGY BLAST MUST HAVE AFFECTED MY POWERS!

THE POSSE!

HEADING MY WAY!

CRUNCH!

I HEARD A CRY -- LOOK OUT!

THERE SHE GOES!

HOW EXTREME IS THE POWER LOSS?

MY ABILITIES SEEM THE MOST AFFECTED -- ORORO'S PSYCHE IS GAINING ASCENDENCY. I FIND MYSELF THINKING IN HER TERMS, REACTING AS SHE WOULD.

SUPPOSE THE EFFECT IS PERMANENT? ONCE HER ABILITIES REVERT, I COULD BECOME A NORMAL PERSON. BUT IF I LOSE HER POWERS AS WELL -- !

SHE'S STILL FLYING!

BUT ERRATICALLY -- THE GUN'S CRIPPLED HER!

KEEP AFTER HER, GYRICH! BRING HER DOWN!

I NEED ALL MY SPEED AND AGILITY!

FOR ORORO'S SAKE, I DARE NOT AFFORD ANOTHER HIT!

15

SINCE I STILL CONTROL HER ELEMENTAL ABILITIES...

...I SHALL PUT THEM TO GOOD USE.

"A SMALL TORNADO SHOULD PROVE SUFFICIENT."

U.S. ARMY

HIT THE DECK!

BWHOOM!

UNFORTUNATELY, NEARBY...

WHERE THE BLAZES DID THIS MESS COME FROM?!

FIVE MINUTES AGO, THE SKY WAS CLEAR--

--NOW WE'RE IN THE MIDDLE OF A FULL-FLEDGED *HURRICANE!*

YOW!

LIGHTNING-- WIND-- RAIN-- THIS IS A REAL *STORM!*

MAYDAY! *MAYDAY!* TUG LONGSHOT ANNIE DECLARING AN EMERGENCY! WE'VE LOST OUR MAIN ENGINE AND WE'RE TAKING WATER!

16

BE CALM, ROGUE. I AM HERE.

ORORO--?!?

THERE-- THE STORM IS DISPERSING.

HOW LONG'VE YOU BEEN OKAY?

MY AWARENESS BEGAN TO RETURN WHEN YOU WERE LAST ON THE BEACH-- I FELT THE LIGHTNING STRIKE.

THAT MEANS THE THOUGHTS AH HAD-- ABOUT THE TUG'S CREW-- WEREN'T HERE AT ALL, BUT MY OWN!

AIN'T THAT A CROCK-- MY REP REALLY IS SHOT!

I BROUGHT YOUR TUNIC.

THANKS!

YOU LOOK-- STRANGELY HAPPY...

JUST COMIN' T' TERMS WITH MYSELF-- CONCEDIN' YOU MAY KNOW WHAT YOU'RE TALKIN' ABOUT-- PERHAPS AH'M NOT AS ROTTEN AS AH LIKED T' THINK.

THERE IS HOPE FOR EVERYONE, CHILD.

IF YOU SAY SO. WHAT'S OUR NEXT MOVE?

THE TUG IS FOUNDERING.

WE MUST TOW IT ASHORE!

18

YOU B'LIEVE WHAT WE'RE SEEIN', JODY?

WIMMIN'S LIB, MAX.

THE FEDS LEFT ME ALONE FOR SO LONG, STORM-- AH WONDER WHAT MADE 'EM SUDDENLY COME AFTER ME?

THEY BELIEVE YOU RESPONSIBLE FOR THE MURDER OF A SHIELD AGENT DURING YOUR RESCUE OF MICHAEL ROSSI.

THAT'S CRAZY! AH DIDN'T KILL ANYONE. THERE WAS A DEAD GUY IN ROSSI'S CELL, BUT HE'D BEEN WHACKED BY HIS PARTNER-- ORORO, AH'M BEIN' FRAMED!

WE BETTER MAKE TRACKS, WHILE WE HAVE THE CHANCE.

THEY'VE GOT A WEAPON THAT CANCELS OUT SUPERPOWERS!

"AN' LOOK-- THEY'RE BRINGIN' IN RE-INFORCEMENTS!"

" I KNOW OF THE NEUTRALIZER, ROGUE. MYSTIQUE TOLD ME WHEN SHE TOLD ME WHERE TO FIND YOU." *

*FOR THAT STORY, SEE FUTURE ISSUES OF MARVEL FANFARE --ANN.

COMPANY, Dr. COOPER!

THAT'S FORGE'S PRIVATE JET!

SPLENDID-- THOSE MUTIES ARE HEADING RIGHT FOR US!

THE CURRENT IS TOO SWIFT-- THE WATER TOO ROUGH-- IF WE ABANDON THE VESSEL AND IT SINKS, ITS CREW MAY DROWN.

OUR POWERS-- OUR PRESENCE-- PLACED THEM IN DANGER, ROGUE!

WE MUST SAVE THEM IF WE CAN, REGARD-LESS OF THE DANGER.

MY MISTAKE WAS USING THE MINIMAL SETTING.

I'VE RECALIBRATED FOR FULL POWER!

19

OH, NO! OH, *NO!*

THERE'S STORM! BUT I CAN'T SEE ANY SIGN OF THE OTHER ONE--*ROGUE*-- SHE FELL IN MID-CHANNEL. THE CURRENT MUST'VE SWEPT HER AWAY.

SHE CAUGHT THE FULL BRUNT OF STORM'S POWER DISCHARGE AND THE SECONDARY EXPLOSION OF THE TUG'S FUEL TANKS. IF SHE SURVIVES, IT'LL BE A MIRACLE.

THE BOAT CREW ARE ALL OKAY, THANK HEAVEN.

TAKE MY HAND, FORGE!

I CAN MAKE IT ON MY OWN, GYRICH. I DON'T WANT YOUR HELP!

I HOPE YOU'RE FEELING PROUD, MISTER--

--YOU JUST SHOT THE WRONG WOMAN!

SHE WAS AIDING AND ABETTING A FUGITIVE!

THEY WERE TRYING TO SAVE LIVES! THEY COULD'VE ESCAPED, BUT THEY DIDN'T!

WHATEVER ROGUE DID, SHE-- AND ESPECIALLY *STORM*-- ARE SUPPOSEDLY INNOCENT UNTIL *PROVEN* GUILTY! THAT'S THE *LAW*, GYRICH!

ONLY FOR STORM, A TRIAL'S SUPERFLUOUS. THANKS TO YOU, SHE'S ALREADY CONDEMNED!

YOU STRIPPED HER OF HER POWERS! YOU'VE *DESTROYED* HER!!

21

AND THERE'S **NO WAY** SHE CAN EVER BE MADE WHOLE AGAIN!

OUTLAWS THEY MAY BE-- IN THE EYES OF THE GOVERNMENT-- BUT THE X-MEN ALWAYS FOUGHT FOR HUMANITY!

BEHOLD, SISTERS, IN OUR MYSTIC SCRYING POOL...

...THE FOREMOST THREAT TO THE *DIRE WRAITHS* YET POSED BY THESE UPSTART MAMMALS.

YOUR STUPIDITY HAS HAS CHANGED THAT. YOU MAY SINGLE-HANDEDLY HAVE TURNED THEM FROM OUR DEFENDERS TO OUR DEADLIEST **ENEMIES**.

THAT MECHANISM IS A PRIMITIVE ANALOGUE TO THE *NEUTRALIZER* USED AGAINST US BY OUR MOST DREAD FOE, THE GALADORIAN SILVER SPACEKNIGHT, *ROM!*

AS YET, ITS POWER CANNOT HARM US, BUT IT IS DERIVED FROM SIMILAR PRINCIPLES. GIVEN TIME, ITS CREATOR WILL INEVITABLY EVOLVE IT INTO A TERRAN VERSION OF THAT ACCURSED GALADORIAN WEAPON.

EVERY HUMAN SOLDIER WILL THEN HAVE THE MEANS OF BANISHING US, AS ROM DOES, TO *LIMBO!*

THAT WE CANNOT ALLOW...

...FOR IT WOULD MEAN OUR DEFEAT-- AND *DOOM!*

THEREFORE-- FORGE MUST DIE!!

NEXT:

BY CHRIS CLAREMONT, BARRY WINDSOR-SMITH AND TERRY AUSTIN

[28]

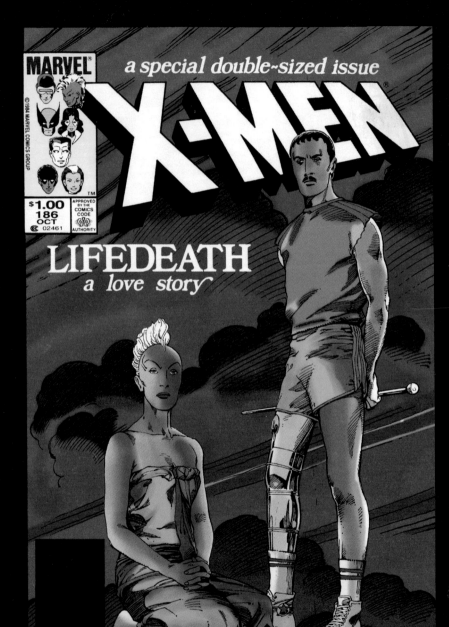

Stan Lee presents the uncanny X-Men

LIFEDEATH

CHRIS CLAREMONT · **BARRY WINDSOR-SMITH** · **TERRY AUSTIN**
SCRIPT —— *STORY* —— *PENCILS* —— *INKER*

WEIN & SCHEELE *colorists* · TOM ORZECHOWSKI, *letterer* · ANN NOCENTI, *editor* · JIM SHOOTER, *editor-in-chief*

ONCE UPON A TIME, THERE WAS A WOMAN WHO COULD FLY.

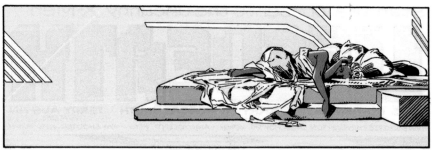

ORORO...

...IT'S FORGE.

HOW ARE YOU FEELING THIS MORNING?

I BROUGHT YOU SOME HERBAL TEA AND HOT BROTH-- MY MOM'S RECIPE, THE CHEYENNE EQUIVALENT OF CHICKEN SOUP.

SHE SWEARS BY IT, GUARANTEES IT'LL CURE ANYTHING.

C'MON, LADY-- YOU NEED TO EAT.

YOU CAN'T JUST LIE THERE AND WASTE AWAY.

ORORO, D'YOU HEAR ME?!

CURSE YOU, WOMAN!

I WON'T LET YOU DIE, NO MATTER HOW MUCH YOU THINK YOU WANT IT!

YOU'RE GOING TO LIVE, ORORO, IF I HAVE TO FORCE YOU EVERY BLOODY STEP OF THE WAY!

GREAT.

HAVE IT YOUR OWN WAY, THEN.

SEE IF I CARE.

SLAM!

TROUBLE IS, I DO CARE.

TOO BLASTED MUCH FOR MY OWN GOOD.

HOW DO I REACH HER?! HOW DO I HELP SOMEONE WHO DOESN'T WANT ANY?!

I'M DOING A WONDERFUL JOB SO FAR. MY PATIENT DOESN'T RESPOND TO THERAPY OR TENDER-LOVING-CARE. NO PROBLEM--

--I'LL SHOVE HER AWAY.

I'VE HURT HER SO MUCH ALREADY, WHAT'S A LITTLE MORE MATTER?

WE'RE TWO OF A KIND, SHE AND I -- *MUTANTS*, THE NEXT STEP IN HUMANITY'S EVOLUTION, BORN WITH EXTRAORDINARY POWERS AND ABILITIES. LUCKY US.

I'M THE *MAKER*. I BUILD THINGS-- LIKE THIS HOLOGRAPHIC DISPLAY SYSTEM.

STORM CONTROLLED THE ELEMENTS.

LORD, SHE'S BEAUTIFUL...

"... WITH A SOUL AS LOVELY AS HER BODY.

" THE PERSONIFICATION OF LIFE ITSELF.

"SHE CHANGED LAST YEAR. HER GODDESS-LIKE SERENITY GAVE WAY TO AN ALL TOO HUMAN PASSION.

"IT MADE HER LOVELIER THAN EVER.

NOW, BECAUSE OF ME...

...THAT'S OVER-- THE BEAUTY GONE FOREVER, THE WOMAN DESTROYED.

SHE WAS LEADER OF THE *X-MEN*, A BAND OF OUTLAW MUTANT SUPER-HEROES.

A FEDERAL STRIKE FORCE WAS AFTER ONE OF THEIR MEMBERS, *ROGUE*, ON A MURDER WARRANT. THEY CAUGHT UP WITH HER ON THE BANKS OF THE LOWER MISSISSIPPI. WHEN I ARRIVED, SHE AND STORM WERE TOO BUSY SAVING LIVES TO WORRY ABOUT GETTING AWAY.

MY MISTAKE WAS USING THE MINIMAL SETTING.

I'VE RE-CALIBRATED FOR FULL POWER!

GYRICH-- *DON'T!*

6

[36]

"I DOUBT ROGUE WAS SO LUCKY.

"SHE FELL IN MID-CHANNEL.

OH, NO!

OH, NO!

"THE CURRENT SWEPT HER AWAY.

I MANAGED TO REACH STORM...

...AND DRAG HER SAFELY ASHORE.

THAT WAS NOT A KINDNESS.

ORORO!?!

YOU SHOULD HAVE LET ME DROWN.

PROFESSOR CHARLES XAVIER'S SCHOOL FOR GIFTED YOUNGSTERS-- IN SALEM CENTER, NEW YORK, HALF A CONTINENT AWAY...

HERR PROFESSOR...?

I'VE TRIED MY BEST, NIGHT-CRAWLER-- CEREBRO HAS AMPLIFIED MY PSI-SCAN TO ITS FULLEST EXTENT--

-- BUT I CANNOT FIND HER.

8

I THOUGHT, USING CEREBRO, YOU COULD PIN-POINT ANY MUTANT ON EARTH?

I SHOULD, ESPECIALLY ONE OF YOU *X-MEN*. BUT I'VE SENSED NOTHING FROM STORM SINCE I WAS STRUCK DOWN BY THAT INCREDIBLE BURST OF PAIN -- A MENTAL SHRIEK OF PUREST AGONY -- THROUGH THE PSIONIC RAPPORT I SHARE WITH YOU ALL.

THE PSYCHIC TRAUMA WAS SO INTENSE, IT RENDERED ME UNCONSCIOUS FOR OVER A DAY, AND LEFT ME UNABLE TO UTILIZE MY TELEPATHIC ABILITIES BEFORE THIS.

PROFESSOR, WAS WHAT YOU FELT...

...ORORO'S DEATH?

I WISH, MY FRIEND, I COULD SAY NO.

HOWEVER, LET'S ASSUME SHE'S STILL ALIVE, AND SOMEHOW SHIELDED FROM MY PROBES. SHE LEFT THE MANSION IN SEARCH OF ROGUE.

I'LL SCAN FOR HER. PERHAPS SHE CAN LEAD US TO STORM, OR TELL US OF HER FATE.

DALLAS, TEXAS...

EAGLE PLAZA...

FORGE, IS THERE ANY WORD OF ROGUE?

9

HENRY GYRICH AND HIS TEAM HAVE BEEN SEARCHING THE RIVER, DOWNSTREAM FROM WHERE SHE LANDED--

-- WITHOUT SUCCESS. SHE EITHER DROWNED OR ESCAPED.

ROGUE IS A RESOURCEFUL YOUNG WOMAN. I WOULD SAY THE LATTER.

WHAT BROUGHT THE TWO OF YOU TOGETHER, ANYWAY? SHE'S A CROOK, PART OF THE BROTHER-HOOD OF EVIL MUTANTS.

NO LONGER.

BESIDES, SHE AND I HAVE MUCH MORE IN COMMON THAN YOU SUSPECT.

SUCH AS?

WHEN I WAS HALF HER AGE, I WAS THE BEST PICKPOCKET AND THIEF IN CAIRO.

YOU'RE KIDDING ME!

NO.

MY PORTA-CONSOLE--! IT WAS IN MY BACK POCKET!

CHILD'S-PLAY.

YOU CERTAINLY HAVEN'T LOST YOUR TOUCH.

I SUPPOSE I SHOULD BE GRATEFUL.

10

[40]

IT IS A HUMAN SKILL -- SOMETHING EARNED-- THE NEUTRALIZER DID NOT AFFECT IT.

FORGE, COULD WE HAVE A FLOOR, PLEASE? I FIND ALL THIS OPEN SPACE A BIT... UNNERVING.

I THOUGHT YOU'D BE USED TO HEIGHTS.

THAT WAS WHEN I COULD FLY.

THERE ARE CUMULUS CLOUDS BUILDING IN THE WEST.

WEATHER FORECAST IS THUNDER-STORMS.

ONLY A FEW DAYS AGO, I WOULD NOT HAVE NEEDED TO SEE THE STORM TO KNOW IT WAS THERE. I WOULD HAVE FELT ITS POWER RESONATING WITHIN ME.

I COULD HAVE TOLD YOU PRECISELY WHEN ITS RAIN WOULD FALL AND HOW MUCH, FOR HOW LONG.

I COULD HAVE NUDGED IT ASIDE. OR GENTLED ITS FURY. I COULD HAVE MADE ITS THUNDER AND LIGHTNING MY OWN.

NOW, I CAN DO NOTHING BUT WATCH.

YOU'RE ALIVE, ORORO. DOESN'T THAT COUNT FOR ANYTHING?

11

I WON'T ACCEPT THAT.

THIS IS NOT LIFE, FORGE, MERELY EXISTENCE-- A SHADOW OF WHAT WAS. TO BELIEVE OTHERWISE IS BUT THE CRUELEST OF DECEPTIONS.

YOU DO NOT UNDERSTAND-- HOW COULD YOU ?! I COULD FLY! I WAS ONE WITH ALL CREATION!

AND NOW YOU'VE GOT TO WALK, LIKE EVERYBODY ELSE. THE GODDESS HAS BECOME JUST PLAIN FOLKS.

TOUGH BREAK.

DUNCE !

EACH TIME YOU OPEN YOUR MOUTH-- WITH THE BEST OF INTENTIONS-- YOU MAKE MATTERS WORSE !

I CAN'T HELP MYSELF. I GET SO ANGRY-- AT ME, NOT ORORO, BUT I END UP TAKING IT OUT ON HER. I'M MAKING THE SAME MISTAKES THE SHRINKS MADE WITH ME-- YOU'D THINK I'D KNOW BETTER.

I WONDER IF IT WAS SUCH A SMART MOVE, LEAVING HER ALONE UPSTAIRS. THE PENTHOUSE IS FIVE STORIES TALL -- ORORO COULD END ALL HER TROUBLES BY STEPPING OFF ONE OF THE HIGH PLATFORMS.

12

HURRY UP, SLOW-COACH!

YOU HAD A HEAD-START, FORGE, AND I STILL BEAT YOU...

...GOING AWAY.

WHAT ARE YOU, LADY, PART-FISH?!

LEMME CATCH MY BREATH-- WHOOF!

YOU'VE A LOVELY LAUGH, ORORO.

YOU SHOULD LET PEOPLE HEAR IT MORE OFTEN.

MAY I HELP--?

I CAN MANAGE, THANKS.

I'VE CERTAINLY GOTTEN ENOUGH PRACTICE.

YOUR LEG...

GREAT FOR WALKING, NOT SO HOT IN THE POOL.

Y'SEE, ORORO, I DO UNDERSTAND.

[44]

IF NOT FOR MY OWN... KNACK AT INVENTING, I'D BE HOBBLING ABOUT ON A STEEL PIN AND WEARING A HOOK WHERE MY RIGHT HAND USED TO BE. I DIDN'T BELIEVE IT AT THE TIME...

...BUT I'M A LOT LUCKIER THAN MOST. TOO MANY BUDDIES CAME BACK UNABLE TO WALK AT ALL -- SOME EVEN TO MOVE--OR THEY CAME HOME IN BOXES.

HOME FROM WHERE?

THE WAR. VIETNAM.

WHAT HAPPENED?

I GOT TOO CLOSE TO A BOMB...

...OR MAYBE, NOT CLOSE ENOUGH-- DEPENDS ON YOUR POINT OF VIEW.

AT THE TIME, I -- I WAS PRETTY DETERMINED, TOO. I TRIED TO DO THE JOB MYSELF.

NO LUCK, THOUGH. I'M STILL HERE.

YET YOU TRIED TO DENY ME THE SAME ESCAPE.

WITH LIFE, THERE ARE ALWAYS OPTIONS, POSSIBILITIES-- HOPE. YOU NEVER KNOW WHAT'LL HAPPEN NEXT-- FOR BETTER OR WORSE.

DEATH MAY BE CERTAIN, BUT IT'S ALSO FINAL. ONCE DONE, IT'S DONE-- THERE'RE NO SECOND THOUGHTS, NO GOING BACK.

15

I THOUGHT THAT WAS WHAT I WANTED. I'M LEARNING DIFFERENTLY. YOU'RE SHIVERING, ORORO.

I... AM COLD.

MY BODY AUTOMATICALLY COMPENSATED FOR THE ENVIRONMENT-- KEEPING ME WARM IN THE ARCTIC OR DELICIOUSLY COOL IN THE JUNGLE.

IT WAS SOMETHING I ALWAYS TOOK FOR GRANTED.

AS YOU SAY, I HAVE BECOME "JUST PLAIN FOLKS."

THE SOONER I BECOME USED TO THAT...

CALDECOTT COUNTY, MISSISSIPPI...

WELCOME BACK, DR. COOPER. HOW WAS WASHINGTON?

LOUSY, PHIL. EVIDENTLY, STORM UNLEASHED SO MUCH ENERGY WHEN THE NEU-TRALIZER HIT HER, SHE BURNED OUT THE MUTANT SCANNER THE AVENGERS GAVE US. CONSIDERING THE CIRCUMSTANCES, I DOUBT FORGE'LL LOAN US HIS.

HE ANGRY?

YOU DON'T WANT TO KNOW. YOUR DAY ANY BETTER?

'FRAID NOT. I THINK WE'VE LOST ROGUE. THERE ARE JUST TOO MANY PLACES ALONG THE RIVER TO HIDE-- OUR NET'S SPREAD TOO THIN.

WHAT ABOUT THAT OTHER MUTIE--THE ONE CARTED OFF BY FORGE?

GYRICH SAID HE'D DEAL WITH HER.

MR. TACT STRIKES AGAIN, FORGE'LL LOVE THAT!

IF THEY SLAUGHTER EACH OTHER...

... IT'LL BE FINE WITH ME.

G'NIGHT, PHIL.

16

SEE YOU IN THE MORNING, DOC.

THE LADY DOES NOT LOOK GOOD.

WORD IS, FORGE PROTESTED TO THE PRESIDENT HIMSELF. GYRICH'S ZAPPING THE WRONG PERSON BY MISTAKE...

... ONLY MADE MATTERS WORSE -- WHAT'S THAT?! I THOUGHT I HEARD SOMETHING!

NOPE -- LOT'S DESERTED.

GETTIN' JUMPY IN MY OLD AGE.

POOR VAL -- SHE SAW THIS ASSIGNMENT AS HER BIG CHANCE. INSTEAD, IT'LL PROBABLY FINISH HER CAREER.

TOO BAD. I LIKED HER.

SHE'S A GOOD BOSS. SHE DESERVES BETTER.

YAWWWN -- I HOPE MARTY'S STILL UP, I HATE EATING ALONE. BEEN AWAY FROM HOME -- AN' HER -- WAY TOO MUCH LATELY...

HUMAN!

17

WHUA--?!!

AAAAAAAAAAAHH...

OUR SORCERY PREVENTED ANY FROM HEARING YOUR OUTCRY, PHILLIP ROSEN. AND THOSE WHO LEARN OF YOUR DEMISE WILL MEET A SIMILAR FATE.

YOUR HUMAN FORM AND MEMORIES ARE UTTERLY REPULSIVE TO ME, BUT BOTH WILL BE ENDURED UNTIL OUR MISSION IS ACCOMPLISHED.

COME FORTH, SISTERS...

...THE FEMALE AWAITS.

NOKNOKNO

I'M COMING!

NOKN

NOKNOKNO

GIVE IT A REST, WILL YOU-- I'M COMING!

NOKNO

FOR PETE'S SAKE!?!

18

PHIL!

AH, SORRY, I, UHM...

..,I WAS IN THE BATH.

ANYTHING WRONG?

WE MUST TALK, VAL.

IT'S URGENT.

SURE-- COME ON IN.

MAKE YOURSELF COMFORTABLE, WHILE I THROW ON SOME CLOTHES.

THAT WON'T BE NECESSARY.

HEY--!!

IN A MOMENT, YOU WILL BE BEYOND ALL EARTHLY CONCERNS.

WHAT'RE YOU TALK-- GASP!?!

YOU'VE SHOWN SUCH INTEREST IN *DIRE WRAITHS*, VAL.

TONIGHT, YOU WILL *BECOME* ONE!

19

NO SHE WON'T, SUCKERS!

SHE'S MINE!

ANOTHER HUMAN!

WHO --?!?

SLAY IT-- AT ONCE!

DON'T'CHA RECOGNIZE ME, DOC -- AFTER ALL THE TROUBLE YOU'VE GONE TO, HUNTIN' ME DOWN LIKE A MAD DOG?!

AH'M ROGUE!!

CHUN...

AN', TRUTH T' TELL, AH REALLY HATE DOIN' THIS. IF EVER ANYONE DESERVED BEIN' LEFT T' HER FATE, VAL DARLIN'--

--IT'S YOU!

20

[50]

BUT, RIGHT NOW, AH NEED YOU ALIVE.

THE FORCE OF ROGUE'S ATTACK QUITE NATURALLY DISTRACTS THE WRAITHS.

VAL COOPER MAKES THE MOST OF HER GOLDEN OPPORTUNITY.

WHEN THEY'RE IN HUMAN FORM...

YYRRRII!

...WRAITHS POSSESS HUMAN VULNERABILITIES.

BEST OF ALL, THEY'RE UNABLE TO UTILIZE THEIR ALIEN POWERS.

OH, PHIL-- IF THIS WRAITH BECAME YOU, THEN THAT MEANS YOU'RE... YOU'RE--!

AH THOUGHT AH'D SEEN UGLY CRITTERS IN MY TIME-- BUT YOU CLOWNS'RE IN A CLASS BY YOURSELF!

THAT WRAITH HASN'T A CHANCE-- THEN IT'LL BE MY TURN.

I'VE GOT TO GET OUT OF HERE-- BUT FIRST I NEED SOME ANSWERS!

WHAT DID YOU WANT FROM ME, ALIEN?! TALK!

NO. IF THIS ATTEMPT FAILS, TOMORROW'S WILL SUCCEED. EVENTUALLY, VAL, YOU-- AND YOUR PRECIOUS WORLD-- WILL BE OURS!

21

FOOL! FORGOT--WASN'T WEARING COSTUME --NO GLOVES! WHEN OUR BARE FLESH TOUCHED--AH AB-SORBED ITS ABILITIES ...MEM'RIES... IDENTITY!

CAUGH!

MONSTER'S SO POWERFUL! TRYIN' T' TAKE OVER! MUST FIGHT BACK--HOLD ON... T' SELF!

BUT WHICH SELF IS MINE?!

HUMANS--

--AH'M HUMAN! --

"-- LESS THAN ANIMALS, FIT ONLY FOR THE SLAUGHTER!"

ROGUE!

I'VE ESTABLISHED A MINDLINK, NIGHTCRAWLER! BUT HER THOUGHTS-- SO ALIEN AND... VILE!

INSATIABLE HUNGER... LUST FOR DEATH... DESTRUCTION...

...OVER-WHELMING... PSYCHIC DEFENSES...

I'VE NEVER SEEN HIM SO SHAKEN. AND IF THINGS ARE THIS BAD FOR HIM...

...HOW MUCH WORSE ARE THEY FOR ROGUE?!

IS HE SPEAKING OF ROGUE OR HIM-SELF?!

PROFESSOR--!?!

DRAW WHAT STRENGTH YOU NEED FROM ME, MEIN HERR! HELP ROGUE IF YOU CAN!

THE CO-ORDINATES, PROFESSOR?! CAN CEREBRO PINPOINT ROGUE'S LOCATION?!

MEANWHILE...

WHAT A MESS! THIS MUST BE WHERE PHIL WAS AMBUSHED!

A CHOPPER--! BUT IS IT FRIEND OR FOE?!

23

IT CAN'T BE TRUE-- THAT *CAN'T* BE WHAT HAPPENED-- IT WAS *ME* YOU WANTED, WHY'D YOU HAVE TO HURT *STORM?!!*

YOU BETTER PRAY SHE'S ALL RIGHT, DOC.

OR YOU'LL BE SEEIN' ME AGAIN!

CHAM!

ORORO GOT INTO THIS MESS 'CAUSE O' ME. AH WANTED TO PULL HER OUT BY MYSELF.

BUT WITH ALL AH'VE LEARNED, AH GOT NO CHOICE.

AH GOTTA TELL PROFESSOR XAVIER...

... AN' GET THE X-MEN'S HELP!

MEANWHILE...

WITH MY COSTUME DESTROYED, I HAVE NOTHING TO WEAR...

... SO FORGE HAD THESE CLOTHES DELIVERED.

I WONDER...

...WHAT HE WILL THINK?

MAY I HELP?

HMNH--

Snik

OW!!!

26

ARE YOU HURT?!

NOTHING...

...SERIOUS-- ORORO?

YES?

YOU LOOK...

WHAT DID YOU EXPECT?

THE COLOR-- IS IT NOT LOVELY? AND I HAVE NEVER FELT SUCH WONDERFUL FABRIC. I COULD NOT RESIST, I THOUGHT IT... I...

...FORGE, YOU ARE STARING.

I...DO NOT KNOW. YOU MAKE ME NERVOUS.

EXCUSE ME, FORGIVE ME, THIS WAS A MISTAKE, I WILL FIND SOMETHING ELSE.

STUPID, *STUPID* WOMAN!

IDIOT! CRETIN! CALL HER BACK! TELL HER SHE'S THE MOST BEAUTIFUL THING YOU'VE EVER SEEN. WHAT'RE YOU AFRAID OF?!

NO, NOT A "WOMAN" AT ALL, BUT A FOOLISH CHILD...

...TRYING DESPERATELY TO IMPRESS.

WHY DO I SO CRAVE HIS APPROVAL?

IT IS NOT LIKE ME. HOW MY BEHAVIOR MUST HAVE MADE HIM LAUGH.

I AM BACK.

THIS IS... MORE COMFORTABLE.

YOU'VE CHANGED.

ORORO, I DIDN'T MEAN TO UPSET YOU BEFORE. IT'S JUST, YOU CAUGHT ME OFF-GUARD.

ARE YOU SO ASHAMED OF WHAT YOU THINK AND FEEL THAT YOU MUST HIDE THOSE THOUGHTS AND EMOTIONS?

SOMETIMES.

I LIKE MY PRIVACY. THERE'S SAFETY IN SOLITUDE, EVEN IF OCCASIONALLY I OVERDO IT.

THEN, MY BEING HERE IS A THREAT? PERHAPS I SHOULD LEAVE?

STAY-- PLEASE!

I WOULD LIKE TO.

27

WHAT ARE YOU PREPARING? IT SMELLS DELICIOUS, LIKE...

CURRY -- BUT ACTUALLY, IT'S NOT, IT'S HYDERA...

HYDERABADI BAIGAN SUBJI, OVER CHAWALI-- OH, WONDERFUL!

YOU KNOW THE DISH?

DOES NOT EVERYONE?

TOUCHÉ.

DINNER'LL BE READY SOON, WHY DON'T YOU POUR US SOME CHAMPAGNE?

I DO NOT DRINK, FORGE.

BE DARING, TAKE A RISK. WHO KNOWS, YOU MIGHT EVEN ENJOY YOURSELF.

I AM DOING THAT ALREADY.

FLATTERY, M'DEAR, WILL GET YOU EVERYTHING.

WHY DO YOU JOKE, FORGE? I WOULD NEVER MAKE SUCH FUN OF YOU.

MAYBE... WE'RE BOTH TRYING TOO HARD.

SURE I CAN'T TEMPT YOU--?

IT TICKLES MY NOSE.

AND MAKES YOUR HAIR STAND ON END.

MAY I HAVE SOME MORE, PLEASE?

YOU'RE MEANT TO SIP IT.

TASTE GOOD?

OH.

VERY.

YOU'RE BLUSHING.

YOU ARE STARING.

SO ARE YOU.

MY HEART IS POUNDING-- I FEEL FLUSHED AND GIDDY-- IT MUST BE THE WINE.

FORGE, YOU ARE AN INDIAN?

28

[58]

CHEYENNE.

HAVE I OFFENDED YOU? IS THIS A FORBIDDEN SUBJECT?!

NO-- NO, OF COURSE NOT. I'M PROUD OF MY HERITAGE.

BUT WHAT I WAS HAS NOTHING TO DO WITH WHO I AM OR THE LIFE I LEAD.

THAT SOUNDS CLEVER.

THE PATH OF DESTINY DOESN'T ALWAYS LEAD WHERE WE WANT. I MEAN, YOU BEGAN AS A THIEF BEFORE JOINING THE X-MEN.

TRUE. DID YOUR LIFE CHANGE AS... DRAMATICALLY?

I BETTER CHECK THE FOOD.

PERFECTO!

MY PARENTS WERE KILLED BY BOMBS. THEY LEVELED OUR HOUSE. MY MOTHER AND I WERE BURIED IN THE RUBBLE. I WATCHED HER DIE.

THAT IS WHY I AM TERRIFIED OF ENCLOSED SPACES.

I HAVE NEVER TOLD THIS, TO ANY LIVING SOUL.

WE'RE A LOT ALIKE.

I PROPOSE A TOAST: TO CRIPS AND OUTCASTS!

LISTEN! DO YOU HEAR-- THUNDER?

THE STORM MUST HAVE REACHED US.

WHY NOT PRESS THE YELLOW BUTTON...

...AND SEE.

GODDESS!

TAKE IT AWAY! MAKE IT GO AWAY! MAKE IT STOP!!

ORORO, GIVE ME THE CONTROL MODULE! OPEN YOUR HAND-- LET GO!

BDIP

IT'S DONE. THE STORM IS GONE. YOU'RE SAFE NOW.

I FELT SO SMALL AND... INSIGNIFICANT... IN THE FACE OF THE STORM'S FURY-- OH, FORGE, I WAS SO AFRAID!

THIS'LL PASS, LOVE, YOU'LL COPE.

THANK YOU. OF LATE-- EVEN BEFORE I LOST MY POWERS--

-- I HAVE BEEN LIVING ON THE RAW EDGE OF MY EMOTIONS... FEELING... REACTING... TO EVERY-THING AS INTENSELY AS CAN BE.

THE FIRST LESSON I LEARNED-- AND A VERY HARSH ONE IT WAS TOO--

--WAS THAT MY ELEMENTAL ABILITIES WERE BOUND UP WITH MY EMOTIONS. THE GREATER MY FEELINGS, THE MORE EXTREME THE ATMOSPHERIC RESPONSE.

TO PROTECT MYSELF, AND THOSE AROUND ME, I CULTIVATED AN ABSOLUTE SERENITY OF MIND AND BODY, SO MUCH THAT I LOST VIRTUALLY ALL AWARENESS OF MY-SELF AS A WOMAN.

A FEW MONTHS AGO, I CAST AWAY THOSE RESTRAINTS. I COULD NO LONGER ENDURE MY SELF-ENFORCED SPIRITUAL CELIBACY...

... SO I REBELLED.

I CUT MY HAIR, CHANGED MY CLOTHES-- LIKE YOU, I DENIED AS COMPLETELY AS I COULD MY OLD WORLD AND SELF AND BELIEFS.

NOW-- WHAT IRONY--THE PROBLEM NO LONGER EXISTS. I NEED NOT FEAR MY FEELINGS FOR THE ONLY PERSON AFFECTED-- THE ONLY ONE AT RISK--

--WILL BE ME.

NOT QUITE.

30

YOU'RE BEAUTIFUL.

YOU ALSO.

WHAT ARE YOU FEELING?

I SOAR LIKE AN EAGLE, AS HIGH AS THE STARS-- I AM... HAPPY.

WOULD YOU LIKE TO FLY, TRULY FLY AGAIN?

WHAT DO YOU MEAN?

THE DAMAGE MIGHT NOT BE PERMANENT. I'D LIKE TO EXAMINE YOU...

A KIND AND GENEROUS OFFER, FORGE, BUT I HAVE NO ILLUSIONS-- MY POWERS ARE GONE, AS IF THEY HAD NEVER BEEN.

PERHAPS THE PROCESS CAN BE REVERSED.

CAN WE NOT DISCUSS THIS LATER--?

SURE-- SORRY-- WHO THE BLAZES IS THAT?!

BR.IPP!

BRIP

FORGE-- NO, YOUR TIMING'S PERFECT, AS USUAL. ALL RIGHT, HANG ON, WHILE I SWITCH PHONES TO MY STUDY.

BAD NEWS?

BUSINESS THAT REFUSES TO WAIT. I SHOULDN'T BE LONG.

HURRY BACK!

COUNT ON IT.

HAVE I LOST MY WITS AS WELL AS MY POWERS? I SHOULD HAVE TELEPHONED PROFESSOR XAVIER AT ONCE, TO LET HIM KNOW I AM WELL AND TO TELL HIM OF ROGUE.

HE MUST BE TERRIBLY WORRIED.

MAKE IT FAST, HENRY, I'M BUSY.

SOMEONE TRIED TO KILL VAL COOPER. SHE'S IN A CATATONIC COMA-- THAT'S ROGUE'S TRADEMARK!

ALIVE! SHE IS ALIVE?!!

31

32

WHOWWLFF!

FORGE-- DID THIS DELIBERATELY, TO TRAP ME-- HE MADE ALL THE PLATFORMS AND STAIRS VANISH!

WRENCHED MY SHOULDER-- HURTS--

--BUT I CAN STILL USE IT.

FOOTSTEPS! IF HE CALLS AGAIN...

...I MUST NOT ANSWER.

THAT WILL TELL HIM WHERE I AM. AT LEAST, WITH THE LIGHTS OUT, HE CANNOT SEE ME EASILY.

THE ELEVATOR IS ON THE PENTHOUSE'S MAIN LEVEL-- BUT HOW DO I FIND MY WAY DOWN WITHOUT BREAKING MY NECK?!

HIS CONTROL MODULE. IF I CAN--

EDITBLIP

YYIII!!

KRAKM

33

GONE! CANNOT HELP FLINCHING FROM THEIR TOUCH-- OR THE BOMBS, OR THE FLAMES-- I KNOW THEY ARE PHANTOMS, WITHOUT PHYSICAL SUBSTANCE...

...BUT THEY FEEL SO LIFELIKE!

WERE THOSE APPARITIONS REAL-- IMPOSSIBLE! YET, COULD FORGE'S IMAGINATION BE SO FOUL AS TO CREATE THEM?!

WHY NOT?

NOTHING ELSE ABOUT THE MAN IS TURNING OUT TO BE WHAT IT FIRST APPEARED...

...HOW FITTING THAT HIS SMILE MASKS A MONSTER'S SOUL.

OH!

OROKO! IN THE CONFUSION, SHE MUST'VE GONE OFF A PLATFORM!

SUCH CONCERN-- NO DOUBT... HE HATES THE THOUGHT... OF LOSING HIS PRIZE SPECIMEN.

IF I GO ON, I WILL ONLY FALL AGAIN. FORGE KNOWS HIS ACCURSED MAZE, NO MATTER WHAT I DO HE WILL FIND ME.

KRRRRRMMMMM

--HELP ME!!

DON'T MOVE, YOU'LL ONLY MAKE THINGS WORSE!

ZZZAATT CCH!

BLESSED GODDESS--HEAR ONE WHO SERVED YOU WELL AND LOVES YOU STILL --HAVE MERCY-

35

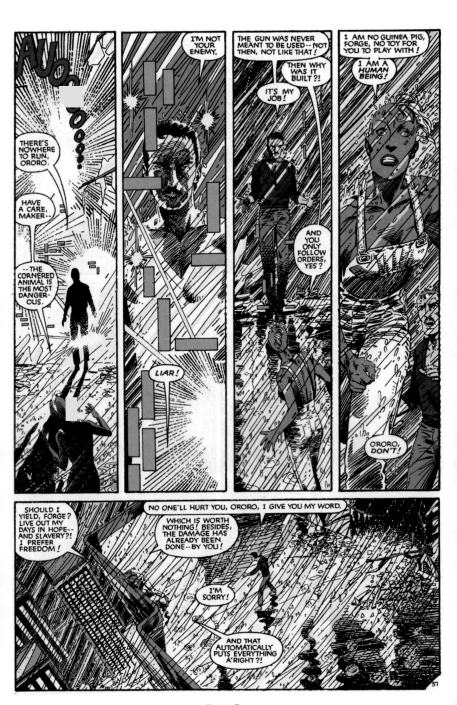

WHAT D'YOU WANT ME TO DO, TURN THE NEUTRALIZER ON MYSELF?! *I* CREATED THE WEAPON; IF THERE'S A CURE, I'LL FIND IT! I'M THE ONLY HOPE YOU'VE GOT!

AN EMPTY GESTURE, FORGE, THE DEVICE AFFECTS ONLY SUPER-POWERS.

MY *MIND* IS MY POWER! I'M JUST LIKE YOU, ORORO-- A *MUTANT!*

OF ALL YOUR LIES, THAT IS VERY NEAR THE CRUELEST.

IF I WAS THE SWINE YOU THINK I AM, LADY, I'D'VE LET GYRICH HAVE YOU FROM THE START!

INSTEAD, YOU HAVE MERELY DELAYED THE INEVITABLE.

I CAN PROTECT YOU!

ARE YOU BLIND? OR DO YOU THINK ME AN UTTER FOOL?!

ALL YOU LEARN FROM ME WILL BE TOLD GYRICH, WHO WILL THEN USE IT--WITH OR WITHOUT YOUR HELP, AND CERTAINLY NOT YOUR PERMISSION--TO SUBJUGATE OR DESTROY MUTANTKIND!

OUR PEOPLE, FORGE! DOES THAT MEAN *NOTHING* TO YOU?!!

WHAT ELSE DID YOU SACRIFICE WITH YOUR HERITAGE: HONOR, DECENCY-- *HUMANITY?!*

AND, TO THINK, I WANTED TO *IMPRESS* YOU-- I WORE THAT SILLY GOWN-- I UNBURDENED MY *HEART!* TO A MAN WHO COULD NOT CARE LESS.

WHO HAS FORGOTTEN *HOW*--IF INDEED HE EVER KNEW.

ORORO--!

STAY AWAY FROM **ME!!**

38

[68]

CHOK

YOU POOR, PATHETIC MAN.

FEEL BETTER?

NO LESS HURT.

NO LESS ANGRY.

YOU LIVE IN YOUR HIGH TOWER-- UNTOUCHED, UNTOUCHABLE-- SURROUNDED BY ILLUSION, SO TERRIFIED OF THE REAL, LIVING WORLD...

...YOU CANNOT BEAR TO VIOLATE THE SANCTITY OF YOUR SPACE EVEN WITH SOMETHING AS SMALL AS A FLOWER.

YOUR HOME IS A TRUE REFLECTION OF ITS CREATOR:

COLD, CRUEL, STERILE--AND, ULTIMATELY, A DECEPTION.

AN IDEAL WORLD WHEREIN THE MASTER OF LIES CAN FEEL SAFE AND SECURE.

39

[70]

WRAITHKILL!

SHE'S SOAKED TO THE SKIN BEFORE SHE TAKES A DOZEN STEPS, BUT SHE DOESN'T CARE.

ORORO ONLY WANTS TO BE AS FAR AS POSSIBLE, AS FAST AS POSSIBLE, FROM EAGLE PLAZA, AND THE MAN WHO LIVES ATOP THIS GLEAMING, HUNDRED-STORY SKYSCRAPER--

--FORGE.

A MAN SHE MIGHT HAVE LOVED.

THE MAN WHO DESTROYED HER.

A STAN LEE PRESENTATION, STARRING THE UNCANNY X-MEN

CHRIS CLAREMONT, WRITER
JOHN ROMITA, Jr. & DAN GREEN ARTISTS
TOM ORZECHOWSKI letterer   GLYNIS WEIN colorist
ANN NOCENTI, EDITOR
JIM SHOOTER, EDITOR-IN-CHIEF

WRAPPED IN BLEAK AND BITTER THOUGHTS-- SENSES DEADENED BY THE TORRENTIAL RAIN--

--ORORO DOES NOT NOTICE A FLASH OF LIGHT FROM THE LOBBY...

...NOR THE CREATURE THAT MATERIALIZES WITHIN.

IT IS A DIRE WRAITH--

--ONE OF A RACE OF SORCEROUS ALIENS, WHOSE GOAL IS THE SUBJUGATION OF HUMANKIND.

ITS MISSION IS TO DETERMINE THE EXTENT AND EFFECTIVENESS OF FORGE'S DEFENSES.

AAAAIIIIIEEEEE

IN THAT, IT IS QUITE SUCCESSFUL.

CLANGALANGALANGALA

AN ALARM--?!

I THOUGHT I HEARD A SCREAM-- BUT IT MAY JUST HAVE BEEN THE WIND.

"NOTHING APPEARS OUT OF THE ORDINARY."

INSPECTOR MATHIS, FBI.

WE'RE ASSIGNED TO PROTECT FORGE.

GLAD T'SEE YA-- IT'S BEEN A WILD NIGHT. C'MON IN!

2

MANY THANKS, OFFICER.

FORGE

WHAT THE --?!

YOU'RE NOT HUMAN !?!

HOW PERCEPTIVE.

POK!

THE BARBED TONGUE STABS TO THE CORE OF JOE HUNTLEY'S BRAIN.

THERE IS A MOMENT OF EXQUISITE AGONY -- SAVORED BY THE WRAITH --

-- THEN OBLIVION...

... AS SHE ABSORBS HIS MEMORIES...

... HIS IDENTITY...

... HIS FORM.

FORGE'S SENSORS DO NOT REACT WHEN THE WRAITH CROSSES THE LOBBY TO THE MAIN SECURITY CONSOLE.

SECURITY

TO THEM, JOE IS AS HUMAN AS HE EVER WAS.

3

THERE IS NO HELP FOR YOU HERE, MAMMAL. THIS PLACE-- LIKE ITS MASTER-- WILL SOON BELONG TO THE *DIRE WRAITHS!*

A CRUMPLED UNIFORM-- A PILE OF DUST-- THE GUARD?!

OH, THE POOR MAN!

BLAM BLAM BLAM BLAM KLIK!

YOU WILL NOT DIE UNAVENGED, MY FRIEND!

YOUR WEAPON IS EMPTY!

AND THOUGH I AM SORELY WOUNDED--

-- YOUR LIFE ESSENCE WILL RESTORE--

PHOOM!

UGH! THE WRAITH-- DISINTEGRATING! BY ALL THAT IS HOLY, THE STENCH IS WORSE THAN A CHARNAL PIT!

IT WAS SHOT-- BUT WHO?!!

NAME'S NAZE.

YOU OKAY, MA'AM?

6

I CANNOT FAULT YOUR TIMING OR YOUR AIM-- THANK YOU.

GLAD T' BE OF HELP. WHAT *WAS* THAT CRITTER, ANYWAY?

A DIRE WRAITH.

AN' YOU'RE...?

ORORO.

THE GUARD'S BODY MEANS THAT THE OTHER PEOPLE I SAW MUST BE WRAITHS AS WELL!

THEY MUST BE AFTER FORGE!

THAT EXPLAINS MY DREAMS.

??

I'M A *SHAMAN.* LAST NIGHT, I SAW THE EAGLE FIGHTING FOR HIS LIFE ATOP HIS AERIE, STRUCK DOWN BY THOSE WHO SEEMED TO BE TRUSTED FRIENDS AND YET, WERE NOT.

THE WRAITHS ARE SHAPE-STEALERS.

AH!

ORORO, FORGE IS THE LAST, BEST HOPE OF MY PEOPLE-- AND PER- HAPS, YOURS --HE MUST BE SAVED.

FORGE--!

ORORO, WHAT--?

GOOD LORD!?!

WHILE ONE CADRE POURS FROM THE ELEVATOR-- FILLING THE AIR WITH THEIR DREAD ENCHANTMENTS...

... ANOTHER STRIKES FROM THE SKY, IN THE GUISE OF FLAME-BREATHING DEATHWINGS.

7

TOO LATE.

SO WHAT NOW?

≡SIGH≡--WE GO TO HIS RESCUE.

BEEN AWHILE SINCE I WAS IN A DECENT SCRAP. I'M LONG OVERDUE.

I HAVE A FRIEND...

... WHO WOULD CONSIDER YOU A MAN AFTER HIS OWN HEART. I WISH HE WAS HERE.

WE'LL DO FINE --

--'SPECIALLY THE WAY YOU SHOOT.

MY FRIEND TAUGHT ME.

WOLVERINE -- I HAVE MY POWERS TO PROTECT ME, AND I HAVE SWORN NEVER AGAIN TO TAKE ANOTHER'S LIFE. WHY SHOULD I LEARN TO USE THIS?

'CAUSE Y' NEVER KNOW WHEN THAT KNOWLEDGE'LL COME IN HANDY, DARLIN'. A GUN'S THE LAST THING ANYONE'D EXPECT FROM YOU.

SOMEDAY, THAT MIGHT GIVE YOU THE EDGE YOU NEED TO SURVIVE.

YOU KNOW FORGE?

YES.

YOU DO NOT LIKE HIM?

NO.

YET YOU ARE HERE, RISKING YOUR LIFE...?

I HAVE MY REASONS.

HIS FATE IS MINE ALONE TO DECIDE.

UNTIL I HAVE MY VENGEANCE, I WILL ALLOW NONE TO DO HIM HARM.

8

THINGS WOULD BE SO MUCH SIMPLER IF I STILL POSSESSED MY ELEMENTAL POWERS -- BUT, THANKS TO FORGE, THAT PART OF ME IS GONE FOREVER. I HAVE ONLY MY WITS, MY STRENGTH, MY... HUMAN SKILLS TO RELY ON.

THAT WRAITH WAS LEFT AS A REAR-GUARD. ASSUMING IT HAD SOME MEANS OF COMMUNICATING WITH ITS COMPANIONS, THEY PROBABLY KNOW OF ITS DEATH.

"I WONDER WHAT SURPRISES THEY HAVE IN STORE FOR US?"

UPON THEIR ARRIVAL ON EARTH, WRAITH SORCERY WAS USED TO MUTATE ORDINARY DOGS...

... INTO DAEMONIC HELLHOUNDS--

--CAPABLE OF DISRUPTING THE FUNCTION OF ANY MACHINE OR LIVING BEING, SIMPLY BY PHASING THROUGH IT.

ARRGH!

IT'S A GLANCING BLOW AND, ALTHOUGH THE EFFECT IS DEVASTATING, ORORO STILL LIVES.

HOWEVER, AS THE CREATURE MOVES IN TO FINISH HER ...

FHOM!

HEYÁ! THESE CRITTERS AREN'T AS TOUGH AS THEY LOOK.

EASY FOR YOU TO SAY! AGAIN, NAZÉ, I AM IN YOUR DEBT.

SAVE FORGE, WOMAN, I'LL CONSIDER US EVEN.

9

SUDDENLY...

ORORO, LOOK-OUT!

WITCH-FIRE!!

BEFORE SHE CAN REACT TO THE OLD CHEYENNE'S WARNING...

...ORORO FINDS HERSELF BOUND, AND YANKED INTO THE AIR!

PAM! PAM!

ORORO!!

THE CABLE--

--ATTACHED TO THE ELEVATOR'S COUNTERWEIGHTS! THEY ARE FALLING-- DRAGGING ME, WITH THEM!

ONLY SECONDS TO ACT BEFORE I AM CRUSHED AGAINST THE TOP OF THE SHAFT-- RIGHT ARM IS USELESS, MUST TAKE THE STRAIN OFF THE LINE --

--MY GUN!

I MANAGED TO SNAG HOLD! IF I CAN UNTANGLE MY LEGS-- PICKING UP SPEED, HOW CLOSE TO THE ROOF AM I?

FORGET ABOUT THAT! I EITHER HAVE SUFFICIENT TIME...

...OR I DO NOT.

10

FREE!

I CANNOT HELP LAUGHING, I FEEL SO-- *ALIVE!*

THIS IS THE SAME MAD, WONDROUS JOY MY FRIEND YUKIO FEELS-- TO RISK ALL AGAINST SEEMINGLY IMPOSSIBLE ODDS--

--AND *WIN!*

TIME TO LET GO. MOMENTUM WILL CARRY ME A BIT FURTHER ON. THEN, BEFORE I BEGIN TO FALL...

...I CAN CATCH A GIRDER...

...AND-- *UNNNFF--* PULL MYSELF TO...

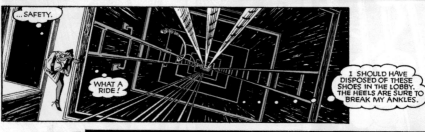

...SAFETY.

WHAT A RIDE!

I SHOULD HAVE DISPOSED OF THESE SHOES IN THE LOBBY. THE HEELS ARE SURE TO BREAK MY ANKLES.

I SPENT MOST OF MY LIFE BAREFOOT. IT STILL FEELS NATURAL TO ME, AND QUITE COMFORTABLE.

NO SIGN OF THE WRAITH-- OR NAZE. I CANNOT WAIT--NOR CAN I HELP HIM-- FORGE NEEDS ME MORE.

BE CAREFUL, OLD ONE. MAY YOUR GODS WALK WITH YOU.

TRAIL'S CLEAR.

I DIDN'T HEAR A BODY FALL, ORORO MUST'VE CUT HERSELF LOOSE-- GOOD FOR HER.

SHE'S A WARRIOR BORN, A MATCH I'D WAGER FOR THE EAGLE HIMSELF. WHAT'D THAT FOOL DO TO MAKE HER HIS ENEMY?!

BEEN AMONG THE WHITES TOO LONG, THAT'S HIS PROBLEM. HE'S LOST ALL SENSE OF COURTESY-- ALL SENSE, PERIOD, LOOKS LIKE.

AH, TO BE TWENTY YEARS YOUNGER-- I'D NOT LET A PRIZE LIKE ORORO SLIP THROUGH MY FINGERS. I'D GIVE MY FOSTER SON A RUN FOR HER HEART...

...HE'D NEVER FORGET!

11

[82]

ONLY EMERGENCY LIGHTS-- SOMEONE MUST'VE SABOTAGED THE BUILDING GENERATORS.

THINGS'LL PROBABLY BE WORSE ON THE STAIRS.

THE DARKNESS MAY HIDE THE WRAITHS FROM MY EYES, BUT NOT MY MIND. I CAN SENSE THEIR PRESENCE WITH MY OWN MAGICKS.

ONE OF 'EM'S *INSIDE!*

PHOOM

PHOOM

YRAIGKH!

GOT IT--

HOKAKEY!!

BE PROUD, MY ANCESTORS! OUR NUMBERS MAY BE FEW, BUT OUR HEARTS ARE STRONG!

COME WHAT MAY, WE WILL PREVAIL!

THESE DOORS-- ICE COLD TO THE TOUCH.

THAT SHOULD NOT BE--!

BRIGHT LADY-- A *BLIZZARD?!?*

IMPOSSIBLE! WE ARE TOO FAR SOUTH -- A TEMPEST SUCH AS THIS SHOULD NOT EVEN OCCUR IN *MIDWINTER!*

FOOL!

I LET MY GUARD DROP--

--THE WRAITHS HAVE FOUND ME!!

12

COME TOO FAR-- FOUGHT TOO HARD-- TO YIELD! OR LOSE!

AIEEE-- THE ACCURSED COLD, IT SAPS MY STRENGTH! I CANNOT MAINTAIN MY SPELLS!

HELL-HOUND-- THE HUMAN IS YOURS!

SLAY HER!

NEED... WEAPON-- BUT VISIBILITY... ALMOST NIL...

WIND-- CUTTING MY SKIN--

-- BLOWING AGAINST ME, CANNOT HEAR ANYTHING FROM BEHIND.

CONSTRUCTION EQUIPMENT! IF I CAN GRAB THAT LENGTH OF PIPE--?!

KTHUD!

HA! THAT DEALS WITH THE WRAITH'S PET!

MY-- HANDS!

THEY FROZE-- TO THE METAL!

LIGHT SUMMER FROCK NO PROTECTION-- MUST GET TO SHELTER-- YARRRGH!

13

I HAVE KILLED-- --WITHOUT HESITATION OR MERCY-- WOLVERINE WOULD BE PROUD.

IS THIS AN ENDING-- THE FAREWELL OF THE STORM THAT WAS-- --OR MY NEW BEGINNING-- OH!

OH!!!

WITHOUT WARNING, ORORO'S MIND IS CRUSHED UNDER AN AVALANCHE OF THOUGHTS NOT HER OWN. SHE IS NO LONGER ORORO-- OR EVEN AN INDIVIDUAL --

--BUT AN AMALGAM OF HERSELF, FORGE, NAZE, WRAITH... AND ONE OTHER THAT IS NEITHER HUMAN NOR ALIEN, BOTH ALIVE AND DEAD, POSSESS-ING THE DIVINITY OF A GOD AND THE CRUEL HUMOR OF THE DEVIL.

SHE FEELS A DELICIOUS TERROR AS THIS MYSTERIOUS "OTHER" THROWS OPEN THE GATES OF CHAOS WITHIN HER-- THEN CRIES OUT AS SHE REALIZES THAT HER SOUL IS GONE. YET, SURPRISINGLY, SHE DOESN'T REALLY MISS IT--

--FOR ANOTHER'S HAS TAKEN ITS PLACE.

SHE REELS UNDER THE MERCILESS PSYCHIC ONSLAUGHT-- DIMLY AWARE THAT, AWFUL AS THIS TRAUMA IS FOR HER...

...IT IS INFINITELY WORSE FOR FORGE.

15

SENSING THEIR PREY'S SUDDEN VULNERABILITY...

...THE WRAITHS PRESS THEIR ATTACK...

... ONLY TO DISCOVER THAT...

...WHILE THE MAKER IS HELPLESS...

...HIS CREATIONS STAND MORE THAN READY TO DEFEND HIM.

THEIR SPELLS INEFFECTUAL AGAINST FORGE'S TECHNOLOGY...

...SOME WRAITHS TRANSFORM TO THEIR DEATHWING PERSONA...

...AND SPRAY THE PENTHOUSE WITH BLASTS OF ACID FLAME.

16

HOLDING YOUR OWN, I SEE.

FREEZE! NOT A MOVE, ORORO, OR I'LL BURN YOU WHERE YOU STAND!

NO REACTION FROM MY SCANALYZER-- YOU'RE HUMAN!

CAN I SAY THE SAME ABOUT YOU?

I SUPPOSE I MUST, SINCE THE BATTLE STILL RAGES.

WHERE ARE THE LIGHTS?

FIRST THING THE WRAITHS DID WAS ZAP THE GENERATORS. EMERGENCY SYSTEMS ARE HOLDING THEIR OWN, BUT I'VE HAD TO DIVERT ALL POWER TO MAINTAIN INTERNAL DEFENSES.

I'M GLAD TO SEE YOU.

WHAT JUST HAPPENED, FORGE? SOME ENTITY BOUND US IN RAPPORT-- TRIED TO DRIVE US INSANE, I THINK SIMPLY FOR THE FUN OF IT!

YOUR GUESS IS AS GOOD AS MINE.

I DOUBT THAT.

HOW NATURALLY YOU LIE. I SHOULD BE USED TO THAT BY NOW.

THINK WHAT YOU LIKE, ORORO, YOUR PRIVILEGE --

--BUT IF YOU'RE NOT HERE TO HELP, FIND A PLACE TO HIDE.

I PROMISED NAZE I WOULD SAVE YOU.

DON'T DO ME ANY FAVORS, LADY.

MY WORD, FORGE, IS MY BOND...

... MUCH AS I MIGHT WISH OTHERWISE--

--TAKE COVER!

ZARK!

17

YOU *MISSED!*

DESPITE OUR CLOAKING SPELLS...

...THE FEMALE SENSED OUR *PRESENCE!* SHE MUST BE *ELIMINATED!*

SHCOM!

SCANALYZER'S WORKING FINE-- BUT THE WRAITH'S CLOUDED MY PERCEPTIONS SO I DIDN'T NOTICE. THAT'S HOW THEY GOT SO CLOSE UNDETECTED.

ORORO'S NO SORCERESS, HOW WAS SHE ABLE TO SPOT THEM?!

UH-OH--THEY CAN DEFLECT MY BLASTER SHOTS!

YOU'VE PROVEN A CONSIDERABLE NUISANCE, HUMAN.

THE HAND BLASTER-- WHERE IS IT ?!!

THIS PUNISHMENT SHOULD PROVE FITTINGLY IRONIC.

THE WRAITH--

--TURNING INTO ME, AND ME INTO ONE OF THEM!

IT'S AN *ILLUSION--*

18

-- BUT HOW DO I CONVINCE FORGE?!

FORGE, THAT WRAITH-- TRIED TO GET ME!

DESTROY HER-- BEFORE SHE CAN CAST A SPELL!

MY PLEASURE!

SFOOSH!

YOU... KNEW THE TRUTH?

IT MEANT CALLING ON A PART OF MYSELF I'VE DENIED FOR TEN YEARS-- ABILITIES I SWORE NEVER TO USE AGAIN--

--BUT I FIGURED YOU WERE WORTH IT.

NAZE!

WE FEARED THE WORST.

OH YE OF LITTLE FAITH--!

WE WERE CAUGHT IN A SOUL-LINK.

IF NOTHING HAPPENED TO NAZE, THEN WHAT TRIGGERED--

I TAUGHT YOU EVERYTHING YOU KNOW, BOY, BUT NOT EVERYTHING I KNOW.

GANGWAY, SUCKERS!

X-MEN COMIN' THROUGH!!

A CONTACT, CLOSE BY!

THE BUILDING--!

IT'S BEEN HIT, BY SOMETHING BIG!

COLOSSUS! ROGUE!!

19

NICE ENTRANCE.

COULDN'T YOU HAVE USED THE DOOR?

ARE YOU WELL, OROR'O?

THE BETTER FOR SEEING YOU, LITTLE BROTHER...

...AND ROGUE.

WE WANTED T' S'PRISE Y'ALL.

WE CAME AS FAST AS WE COULD-- SORRY IT TOOK SO LONG.

HOW DID YOU KNOW WHERE TO FIND ME-- OR THAT I WAS IN DANGER?

"ME AN' VAL COOPER-- FORGE'S BOSS-- HAD A LI'L ... TALK. "

I DON'T WORK FOR HER, KID. I'VE GOT NOTHING TO DO WITH HER OUTFIT.

ANOTHER LIE-- LORDS OF THE EARTH AND AIR!?!

LOOKS LIKE THEY CALLED UP SOME REINFORCEMENTS.

HOW MANY O' THESE YUCKOS ARE THERE?!

FOR EACH ONE WE DEFEAT, A SCORE TAKE ITS PLACE!

MY SPIRIT-SIGHT SHOWS ME THE TRUTH-- MOST OF THAT IS ILLUSION.

BY TRICKING THE X-MEN INTO FIGHTING THINGS THAT AREN'T THERE, THE REAL ALIENS WILL BE ABLE TO CATCH THEM UNAWARES.

IT'S BEEN TOO LONG SINCE I USED MY OWN MYSTICAL ABILITIES--THEY'RE TOO UNDEPENDABLE, I DON'T DARE RISK IT-- I'LL HAVE TO FIND SOME OTHER WAY TO COMBAT THEIR SPELLS.

20

ORORO'S BLASTER...

...DOES THE REST.

A... GUN?! STORM, WHY DID YOU NOT SIMPLY GENERATE A LIGHTNING BOLT?

YOU CANNOT UTILIZE POWERS, COLOSSUS, THAT NO LONGER EXIST.

NO! NO! NO!!

AH WAS HOPIN'-- PRAYIN'-- THAT WOULDN'T BE SO. IT'S *MY* FAULT-- 'RORO SACRIFICED HERSELF T' SAVE ME! *

HUH?!? THE ROOM-- FILLIN' WITH GOLDEN LIGHT, LIKE A SUNRISE!

*X-MEN #185-- ANN.

AND FROM THE HEART OF THAT LIGHT, TWO GLEAMING FIGURES EMERGE...

...CLAD IN SHINING ARMOR.

AAIIIEE -- SISTER, BEHOLD! THE HUMANS HAVE SUMMONED THE SILVER SPACEKNIGHT, ROM-- AND HIS PARAMOUR, STARSHINE!

FACED WITH THEIR ARCH-ENEMIES, THE WRAITHS DISPEL THEIR LESSER ENCHANTMENTS, TO FOCUS ALL THEIR ENERGIES ON THIS NEW THREAT.

WHICH IS PRECISELY WHAT FORGE HOPED THEY'D DO.

22

HOLOGRAMS? WRAITHS HAVE THEIR ILLUSIONS.

I HAVE MINE.

I THINK THESE TWO WRAITHS WERE THE LAST.

THEN WE *WIN!*

PERHAPS-- HAS ANYONE SEEN NAZE...?!

UNNOTICED...

...THE FABRIC OF REALITY TEARS WIDE...

... AND THE BATTLE IS SUDDENLY, UNEXPECTEDLY REJOINED.

ONLY THIS TIME, IT MAY BE OVER BEFORE IT'S TRULY BEGUN.

NEXT: LEGACY OF THE LOST!

STAN LEE PRESENTS

LEGACY OF THE LOST

HOW QUICKLY SOMETIMES THE TABLES CAN BE TURNED.

A MOMENT AGO, THE X-MEN BELIEVED THIS BATTLE WON, THEIR FOES -- A CADRE OF ALIEN DIRE WRAITHS -- UTTERLY DESTROYED. NOW, IT IS THEY WHO STAND IN DEADLY PERIL, AS WITHOUT WARNING, LOATHSOME SHADOWBEINGS ERUPT THROUGH A RIFT IN THE VERY FABRIC OF SPACE ITSELF, TO OVERWHELM OUR HEROES AND BEGIN TO DRAG THEM INEXORABLY TOWARDS THE DIMENSIONAL GATEWAY LEADING TO THEIR OWN SORCEROUS REALM.

CHRIS CLAREMONT, WRITER
JOHN ROMITA, Jr. & DAN GREEN
ARTISTS

GLYNIS WEIN   TOM ORZECHOWSKI
colorist   letterer
ANN NOCENTI, EDITOR
JIM SHOOTER, EDITOR-IN-CHIEF

OUR WEAPONS -- OUR FISTS-- HAVE NO EFFECT ON THESE CREATURES.

THEY DON'T SEEM TO POSSESS PHYSICAL SUBSTANCE.

STORM, USE YOUR BLASTER ON MY ARTIFICIAL LEG. IF I CAN GET FREE, I MIGHT BE ABLE TO FIND A WAY TO HELP US ALL!

THE SHADOWBEINGS SEEM TO SENSE MY INTENT, THEY ARE TRYING TO STOP ME!

CAREFUL, WOMAN! YOU ALMOST HIT ME!

IF I DO-- WHEN I DO-- REST ASSURED, FORGE, IT SHALL NOT BE BY ACCIDENT.

SHE MEANS THAT.

PAL, WHEN YOU MAKE YOURSELF AN ENEMY, YOU DON'T FOOL AROUND.

CONSIDERING WHAT I DID TO HER, THOUGH, IT'S PROBABLY NO LESS THAN WHAT I DESERVE.

WORRY ABOUT THAT LATER. STORM'S GIVEN YOU A CHANCE. DON'T BLOW IT!

I GET THE SAME EMANATIONS OFF THESE SHADOWBEINGS AS I DID OFF THE WRAITHS -- THEY MUST BE MYSTICAL IN NATURE. THEY MERGE THEIR SUBSTANCE WITH OUR FLESH, TURNING US INTO CREATURES LIKE THEMSELVES.

THEY DIDN'T AFFECT ME AS MUCH AS THE OTHERS BECAUSE OF MY METAL PROSTHESIS. DON'T KNOW HOW LONG I HAVE BEFORE THE PROCESS BECOMES IRREVERSIBLE -- I MAY ALREADY BE TOO LATE!

NAZE!

ANSWER ME, OLD MAN, THIS IS NO TIME FOR YOUR IDIOT GAMES. WHERE THE DEVIL ARE YOU, SHAMAN?! I NEED YOU! NAZE?!!

HOWEVER, UPSTAIRS, AT THE VERY APEX OF FORGE'S PENTHOUSE COMPLEX, IN THE CENTER OF A SACRED RING...

HEAR ME, GREAT ONE!

I COME IN HUMBLE SUPPLICATION-- AID MY PEOPLE IN THE HOUR OF OUR GREATEST PERIL.

IN EXCHANGE, WE OFFER THIS WORLD AND ALL ON IT!

-- TO DO WITH AS YOU WILL.

WHA--?!!

FIRE--
EXPLODING
OUTWARDS FROM THE
CIRCLE!

THE
PATTERNS
BEING
FORMED--
I'VE
NEVER
SEEN
THEIR
LIKE--
NO!

MY WARDS--THEY
AREN'T PROTECTING
ME-- BUT THIS IS
IMPOSSIBLE -- IT
CANNOT BE--

--MERCY,
GREAT ONE,
I BEG YOU,
HAVE MERCY!

FOOLISH
MORTAL.

YOU ASK
FOR WHAT I
DO NOT GIVE...

...AND
OFFER
THAT
WHICH I
ALREADY
POSSESS.

YOUR FORM IS WELL KNOWN TO ME,
NAZE, SHAMAN OF THE CHEYENNE--
WE HAVE MET AND FOUGHT BEFORE--

--YET YOUR SOUL, I SEE,
IS CHANGED. IT IS ALIEN.

NO MATTER.
NOW, BOTH
ARE MINE.

3

DALLAS/FORT WORTH INTERNATIONAL AIRPORT-- --ONE OF THE WORLD'S BUSIEST-- COMPLETELY PARALYZED THIS MIDSUMMER NIGHT BY A FREAK BLIZZARD THE LIKE OF WHICH NO ONE HAS EVER SEEN.*

*AND NO WONDER, ITS CAUSE IS THE "CASKET OF ANCIENT WINTERS," COURTESY OF RECENT EVENTS IN *THOR* -- ANN. (BRRR!)

THERE, IN THE FIRST-CLASS CABIN IN A STRANDED TWA 747...

MISS SEFTON! THAT DEMON GRABBED HER AND THEY-- --THEY DISAPPEARED!

BAMF!

AT THAT VERY MOMENT, A HUNDRED FEET OVERHEAD...

NIGHTCRAWLER!?!

ARE YOU *CRAZY*?! HOW *DARE* YOU PULL A STUNT LIKE THAT?!! HOW'M I GOING TO EXPLAIN IT?!!!

PUT ME BACK, AT ONCE!

CAN'T DO THAT, *LIEBCHEN.* YOU KNOW I WOULDN'T HAVE DONE THIS IF THERE'D BEEN ANY OTHER WAY.

YOU SOUND SO GRIM, KURT-- WHAT'S THE MATTER?!

YOU'RE A *WITCH,* AMANDA. THE X-MEN HAVE DESPERATE NEED OF YOUR UNIQUE TALENTS.

I'LL EXPLAIN EN ROUTE.

4

AFTER PROGRAMMING THE X-MEN'S SPECIALLY MODIFIED SR-71 BLACKBIRD AIRCRAFT TO HOVER SAFELY ABOVE EAGLE PLAZA...

... THE GERMAN-BORN MUTANT TELEPORTS HIS LADY-LOVE INTO FORGE'S PENTHOUSE.

THE SIGHT THAT GREETS THEM ISN'T PRETTY.

ZUM TUEFUL--! SAVE THEM, AMANDA, IF YOU CAN!

I'LL DO MY BEST, HON.

MOTHER, WHEREVER YOU ARE, GIVE ME STRENGTH!

HER SPELLS STAB INTO THE CORE OF THE SHADOWMASS...

... PARTIALLY DISRUPTING IT...

....AND ALLOWING SOME OF THE X-MEN TO STRUGGLE FREE.

NOT EVEN THE... BROOD WERE SO FOUL AND... EVIL!

I AM WEAK-- BUT ORORO AND... ROGUE LOOK FAR WORSE. I MUST SEE TO THEM!

5

PETER, GET AWAY... BEFORE-- --TOO LATE!

BY THE WHITE WOLF!!

ROGUE ABSORBS THE ABILITIES AND PERSONALITIES OF ANY LIVING THING SHE TOUCHES-- HER CONTACT WITH THESE HORRORS IS TRANSFORMING HER INTO A *WRAITH!*

HOLD ME TIGHT, MY DEAR FRIEND, I NEED YOU SO. HOLD ME CLOSE--

--THE BETTER I MAY *CONSUME* YOU, BODY AND SOUL!

SHOULD I DO NOTHING, THEN, AND DIE?! THAT IS MADNESS!

JUST THEN...

WHAT A MESS!

SCORE ONE FOR YOU, PROFESSOR. LOOKS LIKE THE BIG BOYS *DO* NEED MY HELP.

WAS-- ?! WHO-- ILLYANA RASPUTIN?!?

BOSHZE MOI! THAT BARBED TONGUE CAN PENETRATE MY ARMORED FLESH! IF ROGUE STABS IT INTO MY BRAIN, SHE WILL STEAL MY THOUGHTS, MY MEMORIES, MY FEATURES-- MY VERY *LIFE!* BUT NOW CAN I SAVE MYSELF--

--WITHOUT MAIMING OR KILLING HER?! THOUGH POSSESSED, SHE IS STILL MY COMRADE. SHE IS NOT RESPONSIBLE FOR HER ACTIONS!

TROUBLE IS, MY MAGICKS AREN'T TOO TERRIBLY EFFECTIVE ON THIS PLANE OF EXISTENCE. THE ONLY REAL WEAPON I'VE GOT IS MY *SOULSWORD!*

ON CUE THE ELDRITCH BLADE APPEARS LIKE ITS YOUN' MISTRESS, SEEMINGLY FROM NOWHERE.

6

THE WRAITHS ARE WITCHES. WE THOUGHT THEM ALL SLAIN-- BUT SUPPOSE WE WERE WRONG?!

THE ROOF, NIGHTCRAWLER-- TELEPORT UP THERE, NOW!

BUT WHY?! AMANDA-- I WON'T LEAVE--!

YOU HEARD THE LADY, FUZZY-- DO IT!

I'M COMIN' WITH YOU!

IF YOU INSIST, HERR FORGE, BUT I WARN YOU...

...IT ISN'T A PLEASANT RIDE.

THAT'S AN UNDER-STATEMENT. I FEEL TURNED INSIDE-OUT!

YOU GET USED TO IT. WHAT'RE WE LOOKING FOR?

STORM FOUGHT A WRAITH UP HERE. SHE LOCKED IT OUT.

BUGGERS'RE EXTRAORDINARILY SENSITIVE TO COLD. SHE FIGURED IT'D FREEZE TO DEATH.

SHE SHOULD'VE MADE SURE.

TOO WEAK FOR ITS SPELLS TO BASH THE DOOR DOWN, BUT STILL ABLE TO GIVE YOUR LADY FITS.

ENJOY YOUR TRIUMPH, MAMMAL, WHILE IT LASTS!

ZASSH!

WE HAVE LAID CLAIM TO YOUR WORLD AND WE WILL NOT BE DENIED!

FORGE, WHAT ARE YOU GOING TO DO?!

DON'T ASK FOOLISH QUESTIONS, X-MAN.

9

TCHAAA-- BE A WHILE BEFORE THIS PLACE IS LIVEABLE.

AT LEAST YOU'RE AROUND TO FIX IT, MEIN HERR.

SOMETHING BOTHERING YOU, MISTER?

CONSIDER ME... SQUEAMISH. KILLING DOES NOT COME AS NATURALLY TO ME AS TO... OTHERS-- EXCUSE ME, PLEASE, I MUST SEE TO MY FRIENDS.

REST, HON, LET MY MAGICKS EASE YOUR PAIN.

PROFESSOR XAVIER WAS MONITORING YOUR SITUATION OVER THE BLACKBIRD'S COMLINK-- OH, ORORO, IS IT TRUE WHAT WE'VE HEARD, THAT YOU'VE LOST YOUR POWERS?!

YES.

I'M SO SORRY!

I, TOO. BUT WHAT HAPPENED NEXT?

I'M A TELEPORTER, KIND OF LIKE NIGHTCRAWLER--THAT'S MY MUTANT POWER-- BUT I'M ALSO A SORCERESS. THE PROF HOPED MY SOULSWORD WOULD MAKE THE DIFFERENCE. I'M GLAD IT DID.

A SORCERESS-- I KNEW YOU HAD CHANGED IN LIMBO, ILLYANA NIKOLOVNA, WHEN YOU WERE BELASCO'S CAPTIVE, BUT I NEVER REALIZED QUITE HOW MUCH.

I WAS MORE THAN THE DEMON- LORD'S CAPTIVE, PETER.

I BECAME HIS APPRENTICE.

WHATEVER YOU WERE, YOU ARE -- YOU WILL FOREVER REMAIN --MY SISTER!

AND, LITTLE SNOWFLAKE, A BRAVER, TRUER, LOVELIER GIRL DOES NOT EXIST ON THIS PLANET -- OR ANY OTHER!

NAZÉ?!?

10.

I SHOULD HAVE GUESSED.

WHAT DID YOU DO, OLD MAN, TRY TO SUMMON THE GREAT SPIRIT HIMSELF?!!

WHY DID I EVER BUILD THIS BLOODY SANCTUM IN THE FIRST PLACE-- DIDN'T I LEARN MY LESSON IN 'NAM?! NO MORE MAGIC--*EVER!*

HOW IS HE?

ALIVE-- BARELY. I'VE GOT TO GET HIM TO A HOSPITAL.

I WISH HIM WELL. WE SHALL BE GONE WHEN YOU RETURN.

NO! I WON'T LET THINGS END LIKE THIS BETWEEN US!

AND HOW, PRAY TELL, O MASTER OF LIES, WILL YOU STOP ME?

ORORO, PLEASE!

DO NOT FOLLOW, FORGE, DO NOT TRY TO FIND US. SUGGEST TO YOUR FEDERAL ASSOCIATES THAT THEY DO THE SAME.

CHEER UP, WARRIOR, OUR STORY IS FAR FROM ENDED. WE SHALL MEET AGAIN.

AND THEN?

YOU MAY WELL WISH WE HAD NOT.

11

HE'S MOVING-- HE'S STILL ALIVE!

COVER ME, PAOLO!

ALEYTYS FORRESTER, ARE YOU CRAZY?!

NO TIME TO UNSHIP THE ZODIAC, I'LL HAVE TO SWIM FOR HIM!

WHOEVER HE IS, HE'S GOT A PASSEL OF SAINTS SITTING ON HIS SHOULDERS.

A GREAT WHITE THAT SIZE SHOULD'VE BITTEN HIM IN HALF!

NO BOAT, NO WRECKAGE--

--NO COAST GUARD ALERTS-- HOW'D THIS GUY GET WAY OUT HERE ANYWAY?!

PAOLO'S SHOOTING-- THE SHARK!

BOOM!

BEAT IT, BUSTER! TRY SOMETHING ELSE FOR LUNCH!

YOU DUMB BROAD, PULLIN' A STUPID STUNT LIKE THAT!

SUPPOSE YOU'D MISSED, THAT FISH'D TAKEN OFF YOUR BLAME LEG!!

DON'T YELL, PAOLO-- AND DON'T CALL ME "BROAD."

GET THE MEDICAL KIT!

HEY, THIS CRAZY SUIT'S MADE O' CHAIN MAIL!

SAVED YOUR LIFE, MISTER.

THEN, I AM IN ITS DEBT...

...AND, I SEE, YOURS AS WELL, CAPTAIN FORRESTER.

LEE, YOU KNOW THIS FELLA ?!

MAGNETO!

13

73°35' WEST LONGITUDE BY 41°20' NORTH LATITUDE--

--OR, ROUGHLY 1300 MILES DUE NORTH OF THE TRAWLER, ARCADIA...

JOIN ME FOR A SWIM, KURT?

I'LL PASS, *DANKE*, ORORO. WATER AND FUR DON'T MIX.

PITY.

THE NIGHT IS TURNING CHILL.

HERE'S YOUR TOWEL.

BLESS YOU! I AM STILL NOT USED TO FEELING COLD.

THE PROFESSOR SAYS YOUR POWERS ARE COMPLETELY GONE.

AS IF THEY HAD NEVER BEEN. THE GENETIC POTENTIAL EXISTS. MY CHILDREN--OR THEIRS-- MAY SOMEDAY COMMAND THE WEATHER, AS I DID.

BUT NOT I.

THIS IS NOT THE END OF THE WORLD, MY DARLING ELF, OR EVEN OF MINE. I AM A GROWN WOMAN. I HAVE SURVIVED...

...I WILL SURVIVE.

ORORO, I ASKED THE PROFESSOR TO CALL A SPECIAL MEETING OF THE X-MEN.

SO?

I AM NO LONGER A MUTANT. THERE IS NO LONGER ANY PLACE FOR ME HERE.

PERHAPS NOT FOR *ANY* OF US.

DO IT AS A FAVOR TO ME, THEN. I NEED YOU BY MY SIDE, THIS LAST TIME MORE THAN EVER!

14

THEY STILL AT IT, RACHEL?

UH-HUH. KEEP YOUR VOICE DOWN, ILLYANA, THEY'LL HEAR.

THE X-MEN AND THE PROF HAVE BEEN IN HIS STUDY FOR HOURS!

THEY CALLED *WOLVERINE* IN JAPAN BUT HE REFUSED TO COME HOME. SOMETHING'S UP-- KITTY'S OVER THERE, TO-- BUT HE WON'T TELL WHAT AND HE INSISTED HE'D HANDLE IT HIMSELF. *

*SEE THE KITTY/WOLVERINE MINI-SERIES, ON SALE NOW--A.

SOUNDS REAL GRIM, I HOPE KITTY'S OKAY.

WHAT DOES ALL THIS MEAN?!

THEY'RE ARGUING, ROBERTO, SO IT CAN'T BE GOOD.

OURS IS A PRIVATE DISCUSSION, CHILDREN.

PROFESSOR XAVIER!

THE HOUR IS LONG PAST YOUR BEDTIME. PLEASE RETURN TO YOUR ROOMS. I'LL ANSWER ANY QUESTIONS IN THE MORNING. GOOD NIGHT.

YOU COMING, RACHEL? WHEN HE USES THAT TONE OF VOICE, HE MEANS BUSINESS.

I KNOW. GO AHEAD, ILLYANA, I'LL BE OKAY.

I'M A TELEPATH, PROFESSOR, JUST LIKE YOU. I COULDN'T SHIELD THREE SETS OF THOUGHTS FROM YOUR PSI-SCANS...

...BUT HIDING MYSELF ALONE IS ANOTHER MATTER ENTIRELY.

I KNOW YOU'LL BE ANGRY WITH ME. I DON'T CARE, I HAVE TO KNOW.

IT WASN'T A SUPER-VILLAIN THAT MAIMED STORM, *HERR PROFESSOR*, BUT THE *UNITED STATES GOVERNMENT!*

IT WAS A TRAGIC ACCIDENT, NIGHTCRAWLER, NOTHING MORE.

WHEN SENATOR ROBERT KELLY'S *MUTANT AFFAIRS CONTROL ACT* WAS INTRO-DUCED, NO ONE TOOK IT SERIOUSLY, YET TODAY IT IS GIVEN A BETTER THAN EVEN CHANCE OF BEING ENACTED INTO *LAW!*

15

WE LIVE IN THE LAST QUARTER OF THE 20th CENTURY-- IN AN AGE WHERE MEN HAVE WALKED ON THE MOON AND, SOME OF US, JOURNEYED TO THE STARS! WE HAVE SPLIT THE ATOM, THE SECRETS OF SPACE AND TIME ARE OURS FOR THE ASKING!

YET WHEN YOU FOUND ME-- NOT SO MANY YEARS AGO-- I WAS BEING HUNTED BY A *MOB*--

--WHO WANTED TO DRIVE A STAKE THROUGH MY HEART BECAUSE THEY BELIEVED I WAS A *DEMON!*

I HOPED JOINING THE X-MEN WOULD MAKE A DIFFERENCE, THAT THINGS WOULD GET BETTER FOR MUTANTKIND. INSTEAD, THEY'VE GOTTEN WORSE.

WE ARE STILL HATED, STILL HOUNDED, BY THE VERY PEOPLE WE HAVE SWORN TO PROTECT.

SO I FIND MYSELF ASKING, WHY?! WHAT'S THE POINT?!

WOULD YOU RATHER FOLLOW *MAGNETO'S* WAY-- BY CONQUERING THE WORLD AND ENSLAVING HUMANITY?!

IN TRUTH, I'D RATHER NOT BE BOTHERED AT ALL.

IF THE WORLD CARES NOTHING FOR MUTANTS, FINE, THE FEELING'S MUTUAL.

WHAT OF THE X-MEN?

WHAT OF US?! FORGIVE ME, BUT WHO NEEDS US, WHAT PURPOSE DO WE SERVE?!

THE SCHOOL, YES, THAT FULFILLS A DESPERATE NEED-- YOUNG MUTANTS MUST BE TAUGHT THE USE OF THEIR POWERS-- BUT AS FOR THE REST, LET THE AVENGERS OR THE FANTASTIC FOUR HANDLE THAT BURDEN.

THEY'RE POPULAR, THEY'RE ACCEPTED. LEAVE US, THEN, TO LIVE IN PEACE.

DO YOU REALLY THINK RUNNING AWAY IS THE ANSWER?!

AT LEAST, I'LL BE LIVING FOR MYSELF-- AND THE WOMAN I LOVE-- INSTEAD OF SOME AMORPHOUS DREAM! DOES THAT SOUND SELFISH?! WELL, I FEEL I'VE EARNED THE RIGHT-- WE *ALL* HAVE! LOOK AT US, PROFESSOR--

--OF THE X-MEN YOU GATHERED: BANSHEE AND STORM, MAIMED-- THUNDERBIRD, KILLED!

JEAN GREY, KILLED!! WHERE WILL IT END?!

16

KURT--! ALIVE, MEIN FREUND-- I JUST WANT TO... LIE HERE AWHILE... AND GET USED... TO IT...

RACHEL...

IT'S IMPOSSIBLE, ORORO-- JEAN GREY *CAN'T* BE DEAD!

WHY NOT, CHILD?

SHE'S MY **MOM!**

I'M SO SORRY, NIGHTCRAWLER. I'D NEVER INTENTIONALLY HURT YOU, YOU KNOW THAT, DON'T YOU? I MEAN, YOU'RE MY FAVORITE "FUZZY-ELF," WHO TOLD ME BEDTIME STORIES WHEN I WAS A KID AND TOOK ME TO THE CIRCUS!

OH, REALLY?

SCOUT'S HONOR!

ONLY-- NONE OF THAT HAS HAPPENED YET. I GUESS NOW IT NEVER WILL.

YOU CAN'T GIVE UP, THE X-MEN ARE *IMPORTANT!* NOT BECAUSE YOU'RE SUPER-HEROES, BUT BECAUSE YOU'RE *MUTANT* SUPER-HEROES!

YOU PEOPLE THINK YOU GOT IT ROUGH? GIMME A BREAK, YOU GOT *NO IDEA!* TAKE A LOOK AT THE WORLD *I* COME FROM...

"... THE FUTURE THAT MAY YET LIE IN WAIT FOR US ALL IF WE DON'T DO ANYTHING...

"... WHILE THERE'S STILL TIME-- AND HOPE!"

SHE OPENS HER MIND TO THEM, REVEALING A LOVELY SUMMER MORNING...

...AS KURT AND HIS WIFE, AMANDA, ESCORT A 14-YEAR-OLD ILLYANA RASPUTIN TO THE SCHOOL BUS-STOP.

THEY NEVER REACH IT...

...AND SECONDS LATER, AN ARTILLERY BARRAGE LEVELS THE MANSION ITSELF.

18

GET DOWNSTAIRS, RACHEL. YOU'LL BE SAFE IN THE DANGER ROOM.

NOT WITHOUT YOU, PROFESSOR!

I CANNOT. I MUST TRY TO STOP THIS SLAUGHTER!

WE MEAN NO HARM! WE SURRENDER!

IN MERCY'S NAME, CEASE FIR--*

"THE SOLDIERS FOUND ME IN THE RUINS, BY HIS SIDE, THE ONLY SURVIVOR.

"THEY USED DRUGS TO NEUTRALIZE MY PSI-TALENT. THE TORTURE CAME LATER, IN PRISON. EVENTUALLY, I WAS SENT TO THE SOUTH BRONX CONTAINMENT FACILITY-- A CONCENTRATION CAMP!

"IN MY PAST, THE ANTI-MUTANT PERSECUTION BEGAN WITH THE ASSASSINATION -- BY MUTANTS-- OF SENATOR ROBERT KELLY.

SOUTH BRONX MUTANT CONTAINMENT FACILITY

"I EXCHANGED THE ADULT KATE PRYDE'S PSYCHE WITH THAT OF HER YOUNGER SELF. SHE SAVED KELLY-- BUT YOU GUYS KNOW THAT, YOU HELPED HER.

*AN ABBREVIATED RECAP OF THE EVENTS OF X-MEN #'s 141 & 142 --ANN.

"THE REST OF US-- IN THE FUTURE-- WEREN'T SO LUCKY.

"WHEN KATE'S MIND RETURNED TO HER BODY, ONLY I WAS LEFT TO WELCOME HER.*

19

[114]

A FUTURE WHEREIN KATYA AND I WERE MARRIED? DOES THAT MEAN THERE IS HOPE FOR US, STILL? IS THAT WHAT I WANT?

WITH RESPECT, RACHEL, YOU'VE PROVED MY CASE. WHAT DO I OWE A WORLD THAT IS WILLING-- *EAGER*-- TO SLAUGHTER ME AND EVERYONE I LOVE SIMPLY BECAUSE WE *EXIST?!*

SHE DIDN'T MENTION ME-- AH GUESS AH WASN'T PART O' THE TEAM. DID AH SURVIVE, OR WAS AH DUMPED INTO SOME UNMARKED, BACK-ALLEY GRAVE?

ALL THAT HORROR-- AN' IT WAS MYSTIQUE'S FAULT. MY FOSTER MOM WAS THE MUTANT WHO MURDERED KELLY.

ALL MY HOPES...

...ALL MY DREAMS--

THANK HEAVEN, IN RACHEL'S FUTURE, I DID NOT LIVE TO SEE THEM TURNED TO ASHES.

FINALLY, THERE WAS JUST ME.

I FIGURED, WHAT THE HECK, 'NOTHING TO LOSE-- MAYBE I COULD TIMESLIP MYSELF BACK A DECADE OR TWO, ONLY PHYSICALLY INSTEAD OF PSYCHIC-ALLY, LIKE I DID KATE, AND TRY TO PREVENT THAT FUTURE FROM COMING TO PASS.

I GOT *WHEN* I WANTED TO GO-- BUT NOT QUITE *WHERE*, 'CAUSE THIS ISN'T THE PAST I REMEMBER. MY ILLYANA SHOULD BE A KID, NOT A TEENAGER. MY STORM NEVER CUT HER HAIR OR LOST HER POWERS. MY MOM...

A LOT HERE IS DIFFERENT, BUT A LOT IS THE SAME. AND SOME... SOME OF IT IS WORSE.

THERE WERE THOSE AMONG US WHO WANTED ONLY VENGEANCE. THEY WANTED THE SCALES BALANCED IN FIRE AND BLOOD, LIFE FOR LIFE! BUT THE X-MEN STOOD FOR SOMETHING BETTER. THEY NEVER LOST HOPE, NO MATTER WHAT.

BECAUSE OF THEM, PROFESSOR XAVIER'S DREAM-- OF A WORLD WHERE NORMAL AND MUTANT COULD LIVE IN PEACE AND FELLOWSHIP, WHERE THERE WOULDN'T BE ANY DISTINCTION BETWEEN THEM--WE'D ALL JUST BE *HUMAN*-- NEVER DIED.

20

IF YOU TURN AWAY FROM THAT DREAM, KURT, YOU'LL DO MORE DAMAGE THAN YOU KNOW. WE MAY BE DOOMED-- OURS MAY BE A LOST CAUSE-- BUT SOMETIMES THE *WAY* WE LIVE AND DIE IS MORE IMPORTANT THAN THE SIMPLE FACT OF IT.

GIVE UP NOW, AND ALL THOSE SACRIFICES-- IN MY WORLD AS MUCH AS YOURS-- WILL HAVE BEEN FOR NOTHING!

WHAT IS THAT CLASSIC SAYING YOU ARE FOND OF QUOTING, KURT?

"WITH GREAT POWER COMES GREAT RE-SPONSIBILITY."

THANK YOU, MY SON, WITH ALL MY HEART.

WANT IT OR NOT. LIKE IT OR NOT.

VERY WELL, PROFESSOR--

--FOR THE DREAM.

21

SOME VIEW, huh, AMARA?

Oh, RACHEL, IT IS BEYOND BELIEF!

THE MOUNTAINS OF MY HOME IN NOVA ROMA ARE MAGNIFICENT WORKS OF NATURE, BUT THIS CITY IS A CREATION OF MAN!

NEW YORK, NEW YORK, THE MOST WONDERFUL TOWN.

TWO YOUNG WOMEN-- BOTH STRANGERS IN A STRANGE LAND-- WHO'VE VOLUN-TARILY TORN THEMSELVES FROM THE LIVES THEY KNEW TO LEAP HEADLONG, ONE INTO THE FUTURE, THE OTHER THE PAST.

BOTH ARE MUTANTS, AND THAT FUNDAMENTAL FACT RULES THEIR EXISTENCE. MORE AND MORE, IT MARKS THEM AS OUTCASTS. MORE AND MORE, THEY-- AND THEIR FELLOW STUDENTS AT PROFESSOR CHARLES XAVIER'S SCHOOL FOR GIFTED YOUNGSTERS-- FIND THEMSELVES FEARED AND HATED BY THE WORLD THEY'VE SWORN TO PROTECT.

AMARA JULIANA OLIVIANS AQUILLA IS A CHILD OF NOVA ROMA, A CITY FOUNDED NEARLY 2,000 YEARS AGO BY A PARTY OF EXPATRIATE ROMANS, IN THE ANDEAN HIGHLANDS THAT SPAWN THE HEADWATERS OF THE AMAZON.

IN A SENSE, HER COMPANION RACHEL SUMMERS HASN'T EVEN BEEN BORN YET. THE NEW YORK SHE REMEMBERS IS THAT OF THE 21st CENTURY.

TWO C

AND THE MEMORIES AREN'T PLEASANT.

IN HER MIND'S EYE, SHE SEES LOWER MANHATTAN BURNING.

THE TWIN TOWERS OF THE WORLD TRADE CENTER LIE IN RUINS. THOUSANDS ARE DEAD, MANY MORE INJURED.

RACHEL'S A TELEPATH.

2

GIRLS OUT TO HAVE FUN!

CHRIS CLAREMONT
WRITER

JOHN ROMITA, Jr.
PENCILER

STEVE LEIALOHA
GUEST INKER

TOM ORZECHOWSKI, *letterer*
GLYNIS WEIN, *colorist*
ANN NOCENTI, *editor*
JIM SHOOTER, *editor-in-chief*
The UNCANNY X-MEN, *stars*

EVEN THOUGH SHE'S OVER A MILE AWAY, ABOARD A NAVY HYDROFOIL, SHE HEARS THEIR SCREAMS, FEELS THEIR PAIN -- AND THEIR DEATHS.

FOR ONCE, SHE IS GRATEFUL FOR THE DRUGS THAT DULL HER WITS...

...OTHERWISE, THE ANGUISH WOULD HAVE PROBABLY DRIVEN HER MAD.

OVER HERE, MUTIE, WE'VE GOT WORK FOR YOU.

3

SO THAT'S A *"HOUND."* I'VE HEARD OF THEM, SERGEANT, BUT NEVER MET ONE BEFORE.

SHE'S THE BEST, SIR.

WE'RE HUNTING MUTIES, RED, SOMEWHERE IN THE UPPER BAY.

FIND THEM!

SHE RESPONDS AS SHE'S BEEN TRAINED --

-- EAGER TO PLEASE.

THERE!

A WOMAN, TWO CHILDREN, UNRELATED, TERRIFIED, WANTING ONLY TO ESCAPE THE NIGHTMARE THEIR COUNTRY HAS BECOME. IN A FLASH, RACHEL IS AWARE OF THEIR EVERY THOUGHT AND MEMORY AND FEELING.

SHE FEELS NO REMORSE, SHE ISN'T ALLOWED TO...

... BUT A PIECE OF HER SOUL DIES WITH THEM.

BUDDABUDDABUDDA

4

GOOD GIRL, RED, I'M PROUD OF YOU.

WELL DONE, SERGEANT! THAT'S THREE LESS MUTIES TO WORRY ABOUT.

SO MANY DIED-- BECAUSE OF ME.

RACHEL, YOU'RE CRYING? WHAT'S THE MATTER, IS ANYTHING WRONG?!

UHM, NO, NOT REALLY-- *sniff*-- GOT A SPECK IN MY EYE, THAT'S ALL.

SHE'S LYING! SHE'S HIDING SOMETHING!

I WANT TO HELP, BUT FOR THE MOMENT, I'LL NOT PRESS THE POINT.

THAT LARGE VESSEL WE SAW UPRIVER, IS THAT THE ONE ORORO'S ON?

YUP.

"THE X-MEN ARE WITH HER, TO SAY GOOD-BYE."

WE SHALL MISS YOU, ORORO.

AND I, YOU, PROFESSOR.

IT'S A SHAME KITTY PRYDE AND WOLVERINE AREN'T HERE TO SEE YOU OFF.*

NORWAY

*THEY'RE STILL IN JAPAN, THEIR ADVENTURE CURRENTLY CHRONICLED IN THE KITTY/WOLVERINE MINI-SERIES, ON SALE NOW-- A.

YOU COULD ALWAYS WAIT TILL THEIR RETURN.

I CONSIDERED IT, KURT. BUT PERHAPS IT IS BEST I LEAVE NOW. I AM HAVING A HARD ENOUGH TIME BIDDING YOU ALL FAREWELL.

IF I HAD TO FACE KITTY, I FEAR I WOULD NEVER GO. AND I MUST.

5

ENOUGH OF THESE SAD WORDS AND FACES! THIS IS SUPPOSED TO BE A CELEBRATION!

CHAMPAGNE, EVERYONE?

YOU'RE MEANT TO SIP THAT.

I KNOW. I SEEM TO HAVE ACQUIRED A TASTE FOR IT.

MAY I HAVE ANOTHER GLASS, PROFESSOR?

ORORO, ARE YOU CERTAIN YOU'VE MADE THE RIGHT DECISION, LEAVING THE X-MEN?

OF COURSE NOT.

BUT STRIPPED OF MY POWERS AS I AM, I AM OF LITTLE USE TO YOU, ESPECIALLY AS THE TEAM'S LEADER.

I CANNOT ASSUME THEY WILL SPONTANEOUSLY REGENERATE, OR THAT SOME MEANS OF RESTORATION MIGHT BE FOUND-- THOUGH EITHER WOULD BE WONDERFUL-- I MUST REBUILD MY LIFE.

AND THE BEST PLACE FOR THAT IS AFRICA, MY MOTHER'S HOME, WHERE I GREW TO WOMANHOOD.

I UNDERSTAND. I WISH I COULD DO MORE.

ATTENTION, PLEASE, ALL ASHORE THAT'S GOING ASHORE...

YOU HAVE BEEN MY TEACHER AND MY FRIEND. THOSE ARE GIFTS BEYOND PRICE-- NOTHING MORE IS NEEDED.

TIME FOR US TO LEAVE, ORORO. BE WELL!

THANK YOU, ILLYANA. I SHALL TRY.

NIGHTCRAWLER, GIVE KITTY MY LOVE.

DO THAT YOURSELF, LIEBCHEN...

...WHEN YOU RETURN.

6

SOUTH STREET SEAPORT, LOWER MANHATTAN...

WHERE SHALL WE GO NEXT, RACHEL?

WE'RE NOT MEETING THE OTHERS TILL THIS EVENING FOR DINNER, THAT GIVES US THE WHOLE AFTERNOON. THERE'S AN EXHIBITION AT THE MET I THINK YOU'LL LOVE -- BUT FIRST, IF IT'S OKAY...

... I'D LIKE TO DO SOME SHOPPING. I FIGURE I'M LONG PAST DUE.

THAT SOUNDS WONDER-FUL, LEAD THE WAY!

AS THE TWO YOUNG WOMEN MEANDER UPTOWN, MARVELLING AT THE CITY'S MYRIAD SIGHTS AND SOUNDS AND SMELLS...

THIS IS THE LAST LOAD, PHIL. I'M TAKIN' A' BREAK.

SURE THING, JAIME.

T'MORROW'S PAYDAY. I'LL BE ABLE T'GET THOSE BOOKS FOR THE BOY--

--HEY, THAT'S MY LOCKER!

LOCKER ROOM

BE COOL, BRO-- OWW!

I AIN'T YOUR "BRO," STEPHENS. I CATCH EITHER O' YOU MESSIN' WITH ME OR MY STUFF, I'LL TAKE IT OUTTA YER SCUMMY HIDES!

NOW BEAT IT, 'FORE YOU MAKE ME REAL MAD!

IT'S THAT NECKLACE.

I NEVER SHOULD'A LEFT IT HERE-- THAT WAS ASKIN' FOR TROUBLE-- BUT I WAS SCARED T' TAKE IT HOME.

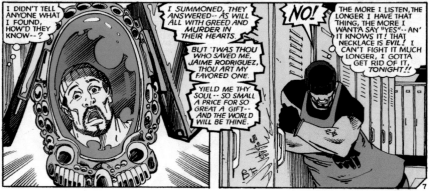

I DIDN'T TELL ANYONE WHAT I FOUND. HOW'D THEY KNOW--?

I SUMMONED, THEY ANSWERED-- AS WILL ALL WITH GREED AND MURDER IN THEIR HEARTS.

BUT 'TWAS THOU WHO SAVED ME, JAIME RODRIGUEZ, THOU ART MY FAVORED ONE.

YIELD ME THY SOUL -- SO SMALL A PRICE FOR SO GREAT A GIFT-- AND THE WORLD WILL BE THINE.

NO!

THE MORE I LISTEN, THE LONGER I HAVE THAT THING, THE MORE I WANT'A SAY "YES"-- AN' IT KNOWS IT! THAT NECKLACE IS EVIL! I CAN'T FIGHT IT MUCH LONGER, I GOTTA GET RID OF IT, TONIGHT!!

7

THE METROPOLITAN MUSEUM OF ART--ON 5th AVENUE AT 82nd STREET--

--QUITE SIMPLY, ONE OF THE FINEST MUSEUMS IN THE WORLD.

RACHEL-- IT'S AS IF I'VE COME HOME!

I FIGURED-- THIS IS A RECREATION OF A ROMAN PALACE. I'M GLAD YOU LIKE IT.

OH, I DO! THOUGH I CONFESS, MY FAMILY'S VILLAS IN NOVA ROMA ARE NOWHERE NEAR SO GRAND.

ROMAN BATHS
HERTAPIUM

I SEE REFERENCES TO CAESARS-- WERE THEY HEIRS TO GAIUS JULIUS?

THE FIRST FEW, ANYWAY. THE OLD REPUBLIC DIED WITH HIS ASSASSINA- TION. HIS ADOPTED SON, OCTAVIAN, BECAME ROME'S FIRST EMPEROR-- AUGUSTUS CAESAR.

MY ANCESTORS FEARED SUCH AN OUTCOME. THAT'S WHY THEY FLED ITALY.

HAD IT NOT BEEN FOR THE NEW MUTANTS...

...NOVA ROMA WOULD HAVE SUFFERED A SIMILAR FATE. MY FATHER WOULD HAVE DIED-- MY OWN FATE WOULD HAVE BEEN FAR WORSE...*

HEY, CHEER UP! EVERY- THING WORKED OUT FOR THE BEST, DIDN'T IT? THE KIDS SAVED THE DAY!

*SEE NM #'s 9-11 --Ann.

I KNOW. I AM VERY HAPPY WITH YOU ALL-- BUT IN MY HEART, I YEARN FOR HOME, FOR THE WORLD AND FATHER I LOVE.

ME, TOO.

BUT AT LEAST YOU HAVE SOME- WHERE TO GO BACK TO. I HAVE NOTHING. NOBODY-- ?!?

8

THOSE THOUGHT PATTERNS-- I *KNOW* THEM!

RACHEL--?!!

HEY!

WHAT ARE YOU DOING, GIRL, WHY ARE YOU RUNNING?!

FOR THEM TO BE SO STRONG, SHE MUST BE CLOSE BY!

THERE-- THAT LIMO!

SHE'S STILL RELAXED, I SENSE NO ALARM. THE INSTANT I RECOGNIZED HER, I PUT A TIGHT LOCK ON MY OWN PSI-PATTERNS. I DON'T THINK SHE SPOTTED ME.

WOULD YOU MIND EXPLAINING...

...WHAT THE DEVIL IS GOING ON?!

SORRY. I MENTALLY "HEARD" A FAMILIAR PSYCHIC "VOICE." IT BELONGS TO A MUTANT WHO VERY NEARLY KILLED ME, NAMED *SELENE*.

PLUTO, IT CANNOT BE--!

YOU KNOW HER, TOO! I CAN SEE THE IMAGE OF HER FACE IN YOUR MIND-- SHE'S FROM *NOVA ROMA*?!

AMARA-- WHY'RE YOU ANGRY AT *ME* ALL OF A SUDDEN?!

MY BRAIN, MY THOUGHTS, ARE MY OWN! I DO NOT LIKE ANYONE SPYING ON THEM, EVEN A FRIEND.

I'M SORRY. I DIDN'T MEAN TO.

SELENE-- THE DEMON HUNTRESS-- KILLED MY MOTHER. IF THAT IS TRULY HER...

...THEN HER LIFE IS *MINE!!*

9

ONLY A FEW BLOCKS FURTHER ON, THE LIMO PULLS INTO THE DRIVE OF AN ELEGANT, VENERABLE MANSION...

FOLLOW ME AROUND BACK, RACHEL. WE HAVE TO FIND A WAY IN.

THIS IS THE SERVANTS' ENTRANCE.

I'VE NEVER SEEN SO MANY ALARMS. IF NOT FOR THE BURGLARY SKILLS ORORO TAUGHT ME -- PLUS MY OWN TELEKINETIC ABILITIES -- WE WOULDN'T HAVE HAD A CHANCE.

IS ANYONE ABOUT?

CAN'T TELL. THE BUILDING'S CRAMMED WITH PSIONIC BAFFLES. I CAN'T PROBE BEYOND THIS ROOM.

I DON'T LIKE IT, AMARA. MOST PEOPLE IN THIS ERA DON'T EVEN BELIEVE IN TELEPATHS --

--YET THIS BUILDING'S GOT DEFENSES THAT'D BE A MATCH FOR PROFESSOR XAVIER.

GO IF YOU WISH.

I AM A WARRIOR AND A ROMAN.

WE DO NOT LET OUR MURDERED DEAD GO UNAVENGED.

WE'RE TOO CONSPICUOUS DRESSED AS WE ARE, WE NEED DISGUISES -- AHA!

NO ONE SHOULD LOOK TWICE --

-- AT A PAIR OF COMMON HOUSEHOLD SLAVES.

A.... COLLAR.

I SWORE I'D NEVER WEAR ONE AGAIN.

RACHEL--? HURRY UP, GET CHANGED!

IT'S EASY FOR YOU TO PRETEND TO BE A SLAVE, AMARA, YOU'VE NEVER BEEN ONE.

10

DESPITE RACHEL'S MISGIVINGS, HOWEVER...

HOW CAN WOMEN EVEN STAND IN SUCH SHOES, MUCH LESS WALK?!

I FEAR MY ANKLES WILL BREAK WITH EVERY STEP!

DON'T LOOK AT ME, PARTNER, THIS LOONEY CAPER IS YOUR IDEA.

I NEED ONE OF YOU LADIES UPSTAIRS, THE OTHER COME WITH ME.

THE BUTLER! I WASN'T EVEN AWARE HE WAS NEARBY! I'LL HAVE TO BE A LOT MORE CAREFUL, I'M TOO USED TO MY PSI-SENSES WARNING ME OF ANY TROUBLE.

HAVING NO CHOICE, IF THEY WANT TO PRESERVE THEIR COVER IDENTITIES, THE GIRLS RELUCTANTLY OBEY.

AT THE SAME MOMENT, IN SECRET CATACOMBS, BURIED BENEATH THE MANSION...

HERR SHAW, I AM FRIEDRICH von ROEHM.

I HAVE THE HIGH PRIVILEGE TO PRESENT, AS CANDIDATE FOR ADMISSION TO THE INNER CIRCLE OF THE HELLFIRE CLUB-- AS ITS NEW BLACK QUEEN--

--LADY SELENE!

REALLY?

I GRANT YOU, von ROEHM, YOUR PROTEGEE CERTAINLY LOOKS THE PART.

BUT THE TITLE OF BLACK QUEEN IS A SINGULAR HONOR, IT MUST BE EARNED.

11

[129]

THAT, MILORD...

...WILL BE MY PLEASURE.

BUT YOU'LL FIND *SEBASTIAN SHAW* IS NOT SO EASILY CAUGHT...

BY HECATE--?!!

MOST IMPRESSIVE, MADAM!

...OR *KILLED!*

HAD I NOT BROKEN FREE, I'D HAVE BEEN ENCASED IN STONE-- AND SUFFOCATED!

MY ESCAPE WAS A VERY NEAR THING.

I ABSORB MY STRENGTH FROM THE KINETIC ENERGY OF BLOWS STRUCK AGAINST ME. THE HARDER I'M HIT, THE MORE POWERFUL I BECOME. BUT SELENE'S WAS A PASSIVE ATTACK, THE KIND MOST LIKELY TO DEFEAT ME.

WAS IT A LUCKY COINCIDENCE-- OR DOES SHE KNOW MY WEAK-NESS?! WHICHEVER, SHE'S MADE HER INTENTIONS PLAIN.

I TOOK THE LIBERTY OF REPAIRING YOUR... THRONE, SEBASTIAN.

AND SITS ON IT AS IF IT'S ALREADY HERS.

AS YOU HAVE SEEN, I HAVE ABSOLUTE CONTOL OVER ALL FORMS OF INORGANIC MATTER. WOULD YOU LIKE A FURTHER DEMONSTRATION?

THANK YOU, NO. THIS WAS QUITE SUFFICIENT.

12

AMONG MY PEOPLE, ON SUCH OCCASIONS, IT IS CUSTOMARY TO PRESENT A GIFT TO ONE'S HOST.

AS A GESTURE OF FEALTY AND RESPECT.

BE PATIENT A SMALL WHILE...

...AND I SHALL RETURN WITH MINE.

KIND WORDS-- FROM SOMEONE WHO FEELS NEITHER.

WHERE DID SHE GO, IS THE WITCH A TELEPORTER?

NO, SEBASTIAN. SHE CREATED A MOMENTARY TRANCE EFFECT-- INSTANT TRANSITORY HYPNOSIS-- THEN SLIPPED AWAY BEFORE WE RECOVERED OUR WITS.

SEBASTIAN, WILL YOU ACCEPT HER?

UNDER THE CIRCUMSTANCES, TESSA, I FEAR I HAVE LITTLE ALTERNATIVE.

THAT'LL BE ALL, YOUNG LADY.

YESSIR. THANK YOU, SIR.

NOT A WORD, RACHEL SUMMERS, NOT ONE BLOODY SOUND-- 'TIL THE DOOR'S CLOSED BEHIND YOU!!!

13

AND THEN... OH MY GOODNESS--*hee, hee*--GRACIOUS-- *ha, ha, ha*--NOT SO LOUD, THEY'LL HEAR-- *ho, ho, ho* -- I CAN'T HOLD IT IN, HURTS--*guffaw*-- HOW *COULD* THEY, I NEVER DREAMED, IT LOOKED SO SILLY, AND THEIR *THOUGHTS,* WAIT'LL I TELL --OH STOP STOP PLEASE NO MORE, IT'S TOO FUNNY, I'LL DIE...

THERE... THAT'S BETTER-- *whews* LISTEN TO ME, WILLYA-- WOW!!

I LAUGHED-- I... I'M *REALLY* LAUGHING!

I CAN'T REMEMBER THE LAST TIME I'VE DONE THAT, I DIDN'T BELIEVE I HAD IT IN ME ANYMORE.

SURPRISE, VAMPIRE!

YOU AMBUSHED ME THE FIRST TIME WE MET*--THAT'LL NEVER HAPPEN AGAIN!

OHWHH!

*X-MEN #183 -- AnnN.

DID THAT HURT?

I'M SO GLAD.

I HOPE THIS HURTS MORE!

TOO BAD THE PLEASURE WASN'T AMARA'S -- SHE DESERVES THIS MOMENT MORE THAN I.

I'M IMPRESSED, SELENE'S STILL BREATHING.

14

WHEN SHE WAKES, RACHEL WEARS HER MAORI MASK, THE STUDDED UNIFORM OF A HOUND-- AND SHE HOWLS IN DESPAIR, FEARING THAT HER DESPERATE FLIGHT TO THE PAST, HER NEW LIFE, HAS BEEN NO MORE THAN AN ILLUSION, A CRUEL PRANK PLAYED BY HER KEEPERS.

AROUND HER LOOMS IMPENETRABLE DARKNESS-- A SQUIRMING AWFUL-NESS THAT IS EVERY THOUGHT AND MEMORY, REAL OR IMAGINED, THAT HAS EVER TERRIFIED HER. THE PERFECT PRISON.

SHE'S TOO SCARED TO THINK, MUCH LESS ESCAPE. SAFER, EASIER BY FAR TO STAY WHERE SHE IS, TO OBEY, TO GIVE UP.

NO! I'LL NEVER BE A SLAVE-- NEVER! FANTASY OR NOT, I DON'T CARE-- I DENY THIS! I DENY YOU!!

I'M STILL MY OWN PERSON, A FREE SOUL-- COMPLETE, IT SEEMS, WITH A FANCY OUTFIT-- SELENE'S SUNK HER FANGS DEEP INTO ME, BUT A PART OF ME IS STILL MYSELF!

BUT WHAT NOW? I'M INSIDE MY OWN MIND, BUT I DON'T KNOW IF I'VE SUFFICIENT POWER TO TAKE CONTROL OF THE REST OF IT AND MY BODY-- AND THE MOMENT I TRY, SELENE'LL SENSE IT AND STRIKE WITH EVERYTHING SHE'S GOT.

WAITAMINNIT-- AMARA'S HER PRISONER TOO, AND I'LL BET IN THE SAME SHAPE I WAS. I NEVER BROKE THE PSILINK I ESTABLISHED BACK AT THE MUSEUM-- CAN I SHIFT MY CON-SCIOUSNESS INTO HER SKULL WITHOUT TRIPPING SELENE'S ALARMS? WORTH A SHOT, ANYWAY-- I'VE GOT ZIP TO LOSE.

16

SCORE ONE FOR ME!

IS THIS AMARA'S IMAGE OF HOME? IT'S LOVELY--EXCEPT THAT, THANKS TO SELENE, IT'S ROTTING AWAY BENEATH THE SURFACE. THE AIR STINKS OF CORRUP-TION--OF HER *EVIL*--BUT AMARA DOESN'T SEEM TO CARE.

AMY-- IT'S RACHEL.

LEAVE THIS PLACE!

YOU DO NOT BELONG HERE-- GO AWAY!

SHE DOESN'T RECOGNIZE ME--SELENE'S INFLUENCE OVER HER IS A LOT STRONGER.

BUT I'M COMMITTED--

-- I CAN'T BACK DOWN-- *WHOOPS?!!*

SORRY, PARTNER--MY TK SHIELDS'LL STOP YOUR MISSILES. YOUR SWORD WON'T EVEN SCRATCH IT.

TOLD YOU.

I'D LOVE TO SPAR, BUT TIME'S OF THE ESSENCE.

FIGHT'S OVER, YOU LOSE.

RELEASE ME!

MAKE ME, BLONDIE!

YOU'RE JUST AN ORDINARY GIRL. HOW'RE YOU GOING TO BREAK MY GRIP, huh?!

EARTH-QUAKE!

NOW OR NEVER--SELENE *HAD* TO HAVE NOTICED THAT, AND, IF I'M LUCKY, THINGS INSIDE AMARA'S SKULL ARE ONLY GOING TO GET WORSE.

HER RAGE IS PROMPTING HER TO DRAW ON HER SUPER-POWERS.

17

[135]

...SO, TOO, IS HER CONTROL OVER AMARA.

I'M BACK IN MY OWN HEAD!

I'M AWARE OF THE WORLD AROUND ME. I'M THINKING MY OWN THOUGHTS-- THIS IS *GREAT*-- AMY BUSTED ME FREE AS WELL, JUST AS I'D HOPED-- *WHOA!?!*

SEBASTIAN, IF THE FIRE-GIRL IS NOT STOPPED--

--HER TREMORS WILL COLLAPSE THE ENTIRE BUILDING!

I'M OPEN TO SUGGESTIONS, TESSA.

SHE'S *YOUR* GIFT, SELENE-- DEAL WITH HER!

IF YOU CAN, SORCERESS-- IF YOU *DARE!*

THE 'QUAKE EFFECTS ARE EVEN WORSE IN REALITY THAN THEY WERE IN AMY'S MIND-- I DIDN'T EXPECT THIS. BECAUSE OF US, INNOCENT PEOPLE MAY BE HURT, EVEN KILLED!

BUT IF AMARA BACKS DOWN, EVEN A LITTLE, SELENE COULD ENSLAVE HER AGAIN--!

PROFESSOR XAVIER, WHEREVER YOU ARE, IF YOU CAN HEAR ME-- OH, PLEASE HEAR ME-- COME A'RUNNIN'!!

IN THE MEANTIME--!

HA! MY PSIBOLT STAGGERED HER! IF I CAN ONLY--!

FOOLISH CHILD, DID YOU NOT LEARN WHEN FIRST WE MET...

...THAT YOUR PSYCHIC POWERS ARE NO MATCH FOR MINE?

AYOWW!

SINCE YOUR WILLS HAVE PROVED TOO STUBBORN TO BREAK, I'LL SIMPLY CRUSH YOUR BODIES INSTEAD.

19

YOUR PARDON, FRAULEIN--

-- BUT WE LIKE OUR YOUNG FRIENDS JUST THE WAY THEY ARE.

NIGHTCRAWLER--?!?

BE CAREFUL, ELF! DON'T GIVE HER A CHANCE TO MINDSHOCK YOU, OR DRAIN YOUR LIFE-FORCE!

BAMF

NO! BRING THE WITCH BACK, SHE'S MINE!

UP AGAINST THE WALL, SUCKERS!

LOOKS LIKE WE'VE ARRIVED IN THE NICK O' TIME, COLOSSUS, AS USUAL.

Y'ALL OKAY, RAY?

PEACHY-KEEN, ROGUE!

THE PROFESSOR'S HERE, TOO--IN HIS ASTRAL FORM-- NOW WE'LL SHOW THESE CREEPS!

IF YOU WISH TO CONTINUE THIS BATTLE, SHAW, THE X-MEN WILL BE MORE THAN HAPPY TO OBLIGE.

WHERE IS SELENE?!

UPSTAIRS, AND, THANKS TO A NERVE PINCH FROM NIGHTCRAWLER, QUITE UN-CONSCIOUS.

I WANT HER!!

NO, AMARA!

YOU WILL DO NOTHING WITHOUT MY LEAVE!

I APPRECIATE YOUR FEELINGS TOWARDS HER, CHILD, BUT MY STUDENTS DO NOT KILL. IF YOU WOULD REMAIN WITH US, YOU MUST ACCEPT THAT.

Y-YES, SIR.

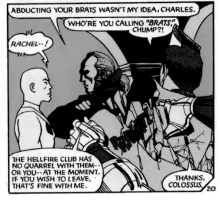

ABDUCTING YOUR BRATS WASN'T MY IDEA, CHARLES.

WHO'RE YOU CALLING "BRATS," CHUMP?!

RACHEL--!

THE HELLFIRE CLUB HAS NO QUARREL WITH THEM-- OR YOU--AT THE MOMENT. IF YOU WISH TO LEAVE, THAT'S FINE WITH ME.

THANKS, COLOSSUS.

20

SOON, IN THE MANSION'S FOYER, AFTER VARIOUS EXPLANATIONS...

WE CAN'T GO OUTSIDE DRESSED LIKE THIS, ESPECIALLY ME AND AMARA.

Y'ALL'RE IN NEW YORK, HON, WHO'D NOTICE?

I DON'T KNOW ABOUT YOU, ROGUE, BUT I'D REALLY RATHER NOT FIND OUT. I'M EMBARRASSED ENOUGH AS IT IS.

ANYWAY, IT'S A PERFECT EXCUSE...

...TO TRY ONE OF MOM'S FAVORITE STUNTS.

SHE USED TO DRIVE DAD CRAZY...

...TELEKINETICALLY TRANSFORMING HIS CLOTHES LIKE THIS.

WHOUOLFF-- I'M MORE BEAT THAN I THOUGHT!

HOW DID YOU KNOW WE WERE IN TROUBLE, AND WHERE TO FIND US?

YOU MUST'VE HEARD MY TELEPATHIC "MAYDAY," RIGHT, PROFESSOR?

NOT EXACTLY, RACHEL.

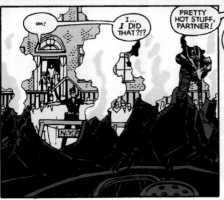

OH!

I... I DID THAT?!?

PRETTY HOT STUFF, PARTNER!

ALL THIS DESTRUCTION -- AND FOR WHAT, MY FRIEND? SELENE YET LIVES, MY MOTHER REMAINS UNAVENGED, THAT ACCURSED DEMON AT LIBERTY TO SPREAD HER EVIL ACROSS YOUR LAND AS SHE DID MINE.

FROM WHAT THE PROF SAID TO MR. SHAW, I BET IT'LL BE A LONG TIME BEFORE SHE STEPS OUT OF LINE AGAIN.

AND WHEN SHE DOES, WE'LL BE WAITING, AND READY, TO NAIL HER ONCE AND FOR ALL.

21

TO MANY, THIS IS THE GREATEST CITY IN THE WORLD.

NEW YORK, NEW YORK.

THE BIG APPLE.

IT IS A PLACE UNLIKE ANY OTHER.

THE STATUE OF LIBERTY

AND NEVER MORE SO THAN TODAY.

An Age Undreamed Of

TWO HUNDRED MILES TO THE SOUTH, IN A CITY SOMEWHAT SMALLER, BUT EQUALLY WELL-KNOWN-- IN A HOUSE WHOSE OCCUPANT HOLDS THE FATE OF THE PLANET IN HIS HANDS...

I'M *VALERIE COOPER,* SPECIAL ASSISTANT TO THE PRESIDENT'S NATIONAL SECURITY ADVISOR. I'LL BE CHAIRING THIS MORNING'S MEETING.

THE ENERGY CURTAIN APPEARED JUST AFTER MIDNIGHT, IN THE CITY HALL NEIGHBORHOOD OF LOWER MANHATTAN.

WITHIN AN HOUR, IT HAD SPREAD TO ENCOMPASS THE ENTIRE ISLAND, ESTABLISHING-- AND HOLDING-- ITS CURRENT POSITION.

OUR MILITARY RECONNAISSANCE SATELLITES HAVE DETERMINED THAT EVERYTHING WITHIN THE CURTAIN-- ANIMATE AND INANIMATE-- HAS BEEN REGRESSED TO THIS BARBARIAN STATE, TRANSLATED INTO ITS EQUIVALENT HISTORICAL ANALOGUE.

POLICE BECAME CIVIC GUARDS, GUNS-- SWORDS, CARS-- HORSES AND CHARIOTS.

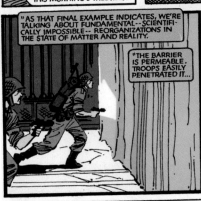

"AS THAT FINAL EXAMPLE INDICATES, WE'RE TALKING ABOUT FUNDAMENTAL--SCIENTIFICALLY IMPOSSIBLE-- REORGANIZATIONS IN THE STATE OF MATTER AND REALITY.

"THE BARRIER IS PERMEABLE. TROOPS EASILY PENETRATED IT...

"...BUT THE MOMENT THEY DID, THEY WERE TRANSFORMED. WE HAVEN'T HEARD FROM THEM SINCE.

"EVIDENTLY, THEY LOST ALL MEMORY OF THEIR TRUE IDENTITIES AND THE WORLD THEY CAME FROM.

NONE OF THOSE AFFECTED VOLUNTARILY WISH OR ATTEMPT TO LEAVE THE ISLAND, BUT SOME HAVE INADVERTANTLY CROSSED BACK THROUGH THE BARRIER. SINCE THAT HAPPENS MOSTLY ON THE RIVERS, WE'VE ORDERED OUR NAVAL UNITS TO KEEP CONSTANT WATCH FOR ANYONE IN THE WATER.

EVIDENTLY, THOSE PEOPLE REMEMBER THEIR EXPERIENCE-- THOUGH SOME DON'T QUITE BELIEVE IT. OUR INTERROGATION OF THEM HAS GIVEN US A FAIR IDEA OF WHAT'S HAPPENING IN MANHATTAN.

4

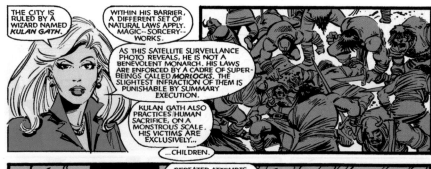

THE CITY IS RULED BY A WIZARD NAMED *KULAN GATH.*

WITHIN HIS BARRIER, A DIFFERENT *SET* OF NATURAL LAWS APPLY. MAGIC--SORCERY-- *WORKS.*

AS THIS SATELLITE SURVEILLANCE PHOTO REVEALS, HE IS NOT A BENEVOLENT MONARCH. HIS LAWS ARE ENFORCED BY A CADRE OF SUPER-BEINGS CALLED *MORLOCKS.* THE SLIGHTEST INFRACTION OF THEM IS PUNISHABLE BY SUMMARY EXECUTION.

KULAN GATH ALSO PRACTICES *HUMAN SACRIFICE,* ON A MONSTROUS SCALE. HIS VICTIMS ARE *EXCLUSIVELY...*

...CHILDREN.

REPEATED ATTEMPTS TO CONTACT *AVENGERS MANSION,* THE *BAXTER BUILDING* HEADQUARTERS OF THE *FANTASTIC FOUR* AND *SHIELD'S* NEW YORK FIELD OFFICE HAVE FAILED.

WE HAVE, HOWEVER, MANAGED TO SIGHT A NUMBER OF SUPER-BEINGS-- WHICH, ALONG WITH THE EYE-WITNESS ACCOUNTS OF ESCAPEES, HAVE CONFIRMED THAT THOSE HEROES, TOO, HAVE BEEN TRANSFORMED.

CAPTAIN AMERICA | WASP | STARFOX | VISION | SCARLET WITCH | COLOSSUS | NIGHT-CRAWLER | STORM | ROGUE

THESE ARE WHO WE'VE MANAGED TO IDENTIFY SO FAR. FOR SOME REASON, *SPIDER-MAN* SEEMS UN-AFFECTED; WE'VE NO IDEA WHY.

THIS... SPELL... DOESN'T ALTER PERSONAL RELATIONSHIPS OR MEMORIES--FRIENDS REMAIN FRIENDS, FAMILIES - FAMILIES, THE AVENGERS - A BAND OF WARRIOR HEROES.

IT'S JUST THEIR EXTERNAL REALITY THAT IS DIFFERENT. THEIR POWERS AND LIVES ARE NOW DEFINED IN TERMS OF THE AGE THEY'RE LIVING IN. THEY BELIEVE THE WHOLE WORLD IS JUST LIKE MANHATTAN.

AND IF WE CAN'T FIND A WAY TO REVERSE THIS ENCHANTMENT OR AT LEAST HOLD IT IN CHECK ...

Dr. COOPER, YOU HAVE *MUTANTS*--THAT OUTLAW GROUP, THE *X-MEN*-- LINED UP THERE ALONG WITH THE AVENGERS AS *HEROES!*

WHAT'S THE IDEA?! WHY, ONE OF THEIR MEMBERS-- THAT GIRL, *ROGUE*-- IS A KNOWN CRIMINAL!

...THEY MAY WELL BE RIGHT.

FILTHY MUTIE VERMIN-- *THIS* WHOLE MESS IS PROBABLY *THEIR* FAULT-- THEY OUGHT'A BE STAMPED OUT, ONCE AND FOR ALL!

5

WHAT DO YOU SUGGEST, JACK, THAT WE HERD THEM INTO CONCENTRATION CAMPS? TEST EVERYBODY IN THE COUNTRY-- MAYBE THE ENTIRE WORLD--AND DISPOSE OF WHOMEVER DOESN'T MEASURE UP?

THE THREAT EXISTS, GENERAL. IGNORING IT WON'T MAKE IT GO AWAY.

HUMANITY IS IN A FIGHT FOR ITS VERY SURVIVAL.

MOST OF YOU ARE TOO YOUNG TO HAVE LIVED THROUGH WORLD WAR II-- OR WHAT THE NAZIS DID. IT'S CALLED THE *HOLOCAUST* FOR GOOD REASON.

I WAS 20 WHEN WE LIBERATED *BUCHENWALD...*

...AND I'LL CARRY THE MEMORY OF THAT AWFUL DAY WITH ME TILL I DIE.

LAST NIGHT, I SAW SOME PIP- SQUEAK RACIST TV COMMENTATOR TALKING IN TERMS THAT WOULD HAVE MADE ADOLF HITLER PROUD-- TELLING HIS AUDIENCE TO BE ON THE LOOKOUT FOR MUTIES, AND IF ANY ARE FOUND...

...AMONG FRIENDS OR FAMILY OR EVEN YOUR OWN CHILDREN, TO *GET RID* OF THEM !

IS THAT WHAT WE WANT FOR OUR- SELVES AND OUR POSTERITY?! IS THAT WHAT OUR COUNTRY'S COMING TO?!!

GENTLEMEN !

THIS ISN'T HELPING. THE PARAMOUNT THREAT WE FACE IS ON THAT SCREEN. BECAUSE THE UNITED NATIONS IS IN NEW YORK, EVERY COUNTRY ON THE GLOBE IS INVOLVED. THEY'RE LOOKING TO *US,* MY FRIENDS.

RIGHT NOW, THE FATE OF THE WORLD, MAY WELL DEPEND ON THOSE MUTANT "*VERMIN...*"

...WHO HAVE NO REASON TO HELP AND EVERY REASON TO WISH US HARM. PERHAPS, IF THEY GIVE US A SECOND CHANCE, WE CAN CHANGE THAT. I HOPE-- I *PRAY*-- SO, WITH ALL MY HEART.

SHE WAKES ACHEY AND OUT OF SORTS...

...FROM A *FITFUL SLEEP* SHOT THROUGH WITH STRANGE AND TERRIBLE DREAMS

SHE SENSES A FUNDAMENTAL WRONGNESS SHE DOES NOT UNDERSTAND AND CANNOT EXPLAIN...

...BUT IS IT WITHIN HER...

...OR THE WORLD AROUND HER ?

ALL SEEMS AS IT SHOULD BE--HAS EVER BEEN--YET IT DOES NOT.

6

ORORO!

WHO DARES--?!

SUNDER-- OF THE VIZIER'S GUARD!

I AM CALLISTO, CAPTAIN OF THAT GUARD.

I HAVE A WARRANT, MY LADY ORORO, FOR YOUR ARREST.

ON WHAT CHARGE?! I HAVE DONE NOTHING!

YOUR EXISTENCE DISPLEASES MY MASTER, KULAN GATH. THAT IS SUFFICIENT.

CONSIDERING YOUR REPUTATION, I EXPECTED MORE RESISTANCE. I'M DISAPPOINTED.

IS THE IRON HOT, SUNDER?

IT'LL DO, CAL.

SPLENDID.

THIS SLAVE-COLLAR'S FOR YOU, WIND-RIDER--

--TO BRAND YOU FOR ALL TIME.

CLOSE IT 'ROUND HER NECK, SUNDER, BEFORE THE METAL COOLS.

NO!

7

YRRAAARRRGH!

THE BRAZIER SET THE DECK ALIGHT! MOST OF THE CREW AND GUARD SHOULD BE TOO BUSY WITH THAT FIRE...

...TO WORRY ABOUT ME.

I'LL MOVE MORE EASILY WITHOUT THESE SILK PANELS ENTANGLING MY LEGS-- BUT WHERE TO GO?! THE FLAMES ARE BETWEEN ME AND THE WHARF, AND CALLISTO IS SURE TO HAVE MORE WARRIORS ASHORE-- WHOOPS!

HE CUT THROUGH THOSE HALYARDS! THE WEIGHT OF THE BOOM IS PULLING THEM UPWARDS!

I SHALL RIDE ONE TO THE MAST-HEAD.

AND PRAY THE CAPTAIN BROUGHT NO ARCHERS.

THE REST OF YOU STAY OUT OF THIS!

THE WITCH IS MINE!

MY MASTER WOULD'VE PREFERRED YOU ALIVE, ORORO.

BUT I THINK HE'LL SHED NO TEARS WHEN I PRESENT HIM WITH YOUR CORPSE INSTEAD!

8

THIS IS A MOMENT I'VE LONG AWAITED, WIND-RIDER. YOU'LL NOT ESCAPE ME NOW!

I HAVE NO WEAPON!

THAT MAKES THE ODDS EVEN.

AFTER ALL, THOUGH WE'RE BOTH MUTANTS, I'M BUT A WARRIOR.

YOU, THEY SAY, ARE A GODDESS!

FOR THE BRIEFEST OF MOMENTS...

...AS PAIN FLASHES ICEFIRE ACROSS ORORO'S BELLY...

...HER WORLD TURNS TOPSY-TURVY. SUDDENLY, SHE'S CERTAIN OF WHO AND WHAT SHE IS--

--AND THAT PERSON HAS NOTHING TO DO WITH THIS TIME.

BEFORE SHE'S EVEN FULLY AWARE OF THE REALIZATION, HOWEVER...

...IT IS OVERWHELMED BY ANOTHER, MORE IMMEDIATE ONE.

THE MAST IS BURNING!

IN ONE SMOOTH MOVEMENT, SHE SWEEPS HERSELF AND CALLISTO OFF THE BOOM.

9

FOOL! YOU'LL KILL US *BOTH*!

PERHAPS.

I MADE SURE CALLISTO BORE THE BRUNT OF THE IMPACT.

SHE IS STUNNED, BUT I DOUBT SHE WILL REMAIN SO LONG.

A CHOKE HOLD SHOULD STEAL BREATH AND SENSES.

IT WOULD BE SO SIMPLE A MATTER TO FINISH THE JOB AND LET HER DROWN. WHY DO I HESITATE? SHE WOULD DO THE SAME TO ME.

NO. WHATEVER I HAVE BECOME, I WILL REMAIN TRUE TO THE WOMAN I WAS.

THE CURRENT-- TOO STRONG TO RESIST-- SWEEPING US TOWARDS MID-RIVER.

GOOD. I WISH TO BE AS FAR FROM THE WIZARD AND HIS GUARDS AS-- *BLESSED GODDESS!?!*

I AM *MYSELF* AGAIN--

--BUT... I WAS NO LESS SO BEFORE.

A MONSTROUS LIE-- YET THE TRUTH! WHAT MANNER OF BEING COULD DO SUCH A THING-- AND WHY?!

CALLISTO SPOKE OF A SORCERER NAMED *KULAN GATH*-- IS *THIS* HIS DOING?!

AND WHAT OF THE X-MEN WHO WERE IN MAN-HATTAN LAST NIGHT?! WERE THEY CURSED AS WELL?!

WHAT HAS HAPPENED TO *THEM*?!!

10

BRING FORTH THE PRISONERS.

THEY ARE BUT CHILDREN-- HOW DELIGHTFUL!

YOUR MENTOR, CHARLES XAVIER, IS ALREADY IN MY SERVICE. INDEED, IT WAS HE WHO LED YOU TO ME.

PROFESSOR'S PSI-POWERS SUMMONED NEW MUTANTS--HE LURED FRIENDS AND SELF INTO A TRAP.

SELF CONFUSED-- FRIENDS UNDERWENT PHYSIO-PSYCHOLOGICAL METAMORPHOSIS, WHY NOT SELF?! INSUFFICIENT DATA-- OBSERVATION, ANALYSIS CONTINUING.

XAVIER INFORMS ME YOU ARE CALLED MUTANTS, FEARED AND HATED BY THOSE WHO LACK YOUR SPECIAL ABILITIES. THAT MAKES YOU MOST PRECIOUS TO ME.

I AM KULAN GATH...

...SOON TO BE MASTER OF THE WORLD!

YOU--AND YOUR FELLOW MUTANTS--WILL PROVIDE THE NUCLEUS OF MY HELLHORDE!

YOU ARE OUTCASTS, AFRAID AND RESENTFUL NO MATTER HOW HARD YOU TRY TO HIDE OR DENY IT.

SEE HOW EASILY I TAKE THOSE NEGATIVE EMOTIONS AND COMBINE THEIR DARKLING POTENTIAL WITH MY OWN POWERS TO RESHAPE YOU BODY AND SOUL!

BY THE MAKER!

12

FORGIVE SELF, RAHNE. YOU WERE SELF'S FIRST FRIEND-- SELF OWES LIFE TO YOU.

SELF SHOULD HAVE ACTED SOONER! BUT THERE IS STILL TIME TO SAVE THE OTHERS!

THE FEATURES OF A HANDSOME YOUNG MAN VANISH, REPLACED BY WARLOCK'S TRUE APPEARANCE.

THOUGH HE IS AS MUCH A MUTANT AS HIS TEAMMATES...

...HE IS NOT HUMAN, NOR EVEN OF EARTH. A METAMORPH-- ABLE TO TRANSFORM HIS BODY INTO ANYTHING-- HE IS A TECHNO-ORGANIC BEING, COMPOSED OF LIVING ELECTRONIC CIRCUITRY.

UNFORTUNATELY, FAST AS HE IS...

...KULAN GATH IS FASTER.

DANI, ROBERTO, SAM-- THEY CHANGE AS WELL!

SELF DARES NOT FIGHT.

THEY COULD DO SELF GRIEVOUS HARM-- WORSE, SELF MIGHT DO THE SAME TO THEM. BETTER TO FLEE...

...AS SELF ALWAYS DOES, TO SELF'S ETERNAL SHAME.

THAT CREATURE'S TERROR AND LONELINESS IS AT LEAST AS GREAT AS ITS FELLOWS-- I SHOULD HAVE ENSLAVED HIM WITH EASE.

IT WAS UNAFFECTED BY MY MASTER SPELL AS WELL. XAVIER-- COME FORTH!

I/ CALIBAN HEAR, DREAD LORD, AND OBEY.

13

EXPLAIN THAT CREATURE'S IMMUNITY.

FIND IT, AT ONCE!

CANNOT. POSSIBLY. IT IS WARLOCK'S ALIEN NATURE. HE IS NOT OF THIS WORLD.

NO.

CALIBAN... WISHES TO OBEY.

BUT-- I DO NOT!

YOUR WILL, LITTLE MAN...

...IS AS FORMIDABLE AS ANY I'VE ENCOUNTERED.

IN YOUR OWN WORLD, YOUR PROPER TIME, YOUR TRUE IDENTITY, YOU MIGHT PROVE MY EQUAL.

BUT MY MAGICKS HAVE RESHAPED REALITY IN MY IMAGE! EVERYTHING --EVERYONE-- IN IT IS MY CREATION!

I...

...HEAR.

I / CALIBAN... OBEY.

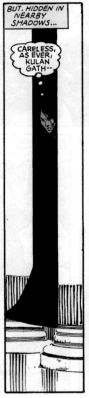

BUT, HIDDEN IN NEARBY SHADOWS...

CARELESS, AS EVER, KULAN GATH--

--YOUR ENCHANTMENT HAS NO EFFECT ON A SORCERESS...

...WHO WAS OLD--HER POWER FEARED-- WHEN THIS WORLD WAS IN ITS INFANCY.

14

UPTOWN...

A PAIR O' PRETTIES FOR THE WIZARD.

WON'T BE SO PRETTY ONCE HE'S DONE WITH 'EM. KIND OF A SHAME, DON'T'CHA THINK, BUCKOS?

WE MEAN NO HARM -- WE HAVE DONE NO WRONG -- TO YOU OR YOUR MASTER.

LET US GO.

WE FOUGHT, RED, YOU LOST. TOUGH BREAK.

NOT SO HASTY, DOLT. NOT ALL MORLOCKS ARE AS HARD-HEARTED AS CALLISTO. YOU BE NICE TO US, SWEET-UMS.

MAYBE WE'LL BE NICE TO YOU.

SUCH A NOBLE OFFER, FROM SUCH NOBLE MEN.

IT SEEMS ALMOST A SHAME...

...TO STEAL YOUR LIVES AND SOULS.

THE STREET -- IT'S COME ALIVE!

I CAN'T MOVE!!

MY DOING.

BUT FEAR NOT, I SHAN'T KEEP YOU PRISONER LONG.

WE MEET AGAIN, DEAR CHILDREN, BUT I'LL WAGER -- THANKS TO THAT IDIOT KULAN GATH'S SPELL -- NEITHER OF YOU REMEMBERS.

PRINCESS AMARA, LADY RACHEL -- I AM SELENE!

15

HOBOKEN-- JUST ACROSS THE HUDSON RIVER...

HOW DO YOU FEEL, CALLISTO?

FURIOUS. I HATE OWING MY LIFE TO YOU.

BUT THERE AREN'T WORDS TO DESCRIBE MY FEELINGS FOR KULAN GATH. NOBODY-- NOBODY TURNS ME AND MINE INTO TOYS!

WHAT THEN DO WE DO ABOUT IT?

DOOR'S LOCKED. THE FEDS MUST MEAN TO KEEP US ON ICE TILL THEY'RE READY TO INTERRO- GATE US.

STORM, CALLISTO--!

A PSICALL-- BUT WHO--?!

SELENE!

HER CLOTHES-- THEY ARE REMINIS- CENT OF THE GARB WORN BY THE HELLFIRE CLUB'S BLACK QUEEN!

I AM USING RACHEL'S TELEPATHIC ABILITIES TO PROJECT MY THOUGHTS...

WITCH, IF YOU HAVE HARMED HER--!

I HAVE NOT. LET THERE BE PEACE BETWEEN US, WIND RIDER. I NEED YOUR AID.

THE ENSORCELLMENT OF YOUR CITY IS THE WORK OF AN OLD AND DEADLY FOE.

IF HE IS NOT STOPPED, AND SOON, HIS SPELL WILL BECOME IRREVERSIBLE-- AND WILL SPREAD FROM THIS SOURCE TO ENGULF THE ENTIRE PLANET!

WILL YOU ALLOW THAT, OR WAS I WRONG IN MY ESTIMATION OF YOUR COURAGE AND SENSE OF DUTY?!

HIS SPELL MADE ME A SLAVE, SWEETHEART. ONCE I CROSS HIS BARRIER, I'LL REVERT-- I WON'T BE MUCH USE TO YOU THEN.

I CAN REMEDY THAT SOMEWHAT, BY USING MY OWN SORCERY TO PROTECT YOU FROM HIS INFLUENCE. AND WHILE YOU WILL FORGET THIS MODERN WORLD AND YOUR ROLES IN IT...

...YOU'LL REMEMBER THE ESSENCE OF OUR CONVERSATION-- THAT KULAN GATH IS AN EVIL WHICH MUST BE DESTROYED...

...AND THAT SELENE IS EVER YOUR FRIEND AND ALLY.

16

YOU BELIEVE HER ?

NO.

TRUST HER?

NEVER.

QUIT SHOWING OFF, ORORO. WHY DON'T YOU USE YOUR ELEMENTAL POWERS TO FLY US OUT OF HERE?

THEY NO LONGER EXIST, CALLISTO.

HOW?! WHAT HAPPENED?!

THAT IS NOT IMPORTANT.

IT IS TO ME.

I DID NOT KNOW YOU CARED.

YOU WON MY PLACE IN FAIR COMBAT AS LEADER OF THE MORLOCKS.

I WANTED TO TAKE IT BACK THE SAME WAY. THAT MEANS NOTHING IF YOU'RE JUST A HUMAN.

MORE IMPORTANTLY, WE TAKE CARE OF OUR OWN. IF SOMEONE DID THIS TO YOU -- AND YOU DON'T TAKE HIS LIFE--

--I WILL.

HEY, YOU TWO-- HOLD IT! STAY WHERE YOU ARE!!

RUN!

SECURITY ALERT-- GET AFTER 'EM! DON'T LET THOSE WOMEN ESCAPE!

WHICH WAY, CALLISTO?

DOWN THE LADDER. ONCE WE'RE IN THE SEWERS, THEY'LL NEVER CATCH US!

OUR MORLOCK TUNNELS EXTEND TO THIS SIDE OF THE RIVER. WE'LL USE THEM TO CROSS BACK INTO MANHATTAN.

MEANWHILE...

< THIS IS CRAZY! NOT ONLY HAS MY HOMETOWN TURNED INTO A GIANT-SIZED SET FROM "CONAN THE BARBARIAN"...>

<...BUT IT LOOKS LIKE EVERYBODY'S FAVORITE PASTIME'S BECOME COLLECTING THE SCALP...>

<...OF YOUR FRIENDLY NEIGHBORHOOD SPIDER-MAN!!>

17

< I'M MOVING AS FAST AS I CAN, BUT I'M NOT SHAKING THESE GUYS. WHAT GIVES? >

< MAYBE I'LL HAVE BETTER LUCK IN A CROWD. >

< GANGWAY! >

WHAT THE DEVILS?!

< OH, GREAT, NOBODY SPEAKS ENGLISH ANYMORE. >

< THE LANGUAGE SOUNDS AWFULLY FAMILIAR, THOUGH-- I'VE HEARD IT BEFORE BUT-- >

WHOOPS!

< BLESS YOU, SPIDEY-SENSE. THE LATEST IN A HOPEFULLY NEVER-ENDING SERIES OF TIMELY WARNINGS. >

< I DON'T DARE HIT BACK TOO HARD. THESE AREN'T REAL VILLAINS, JUST ORDINARY PEOPLE --VICTIMS. SOME OF 'EM MIGHT EVEN BE MY FRIENDS. >

< HEY, I'D KNOW THOSE EARS ANY- WHERE-- THAT'S CANNON- BALL! >

< I'M BEING CHASED BY THE NEW MUTANTS!!* >

*WHOM SPIDEY MET IN MTU ANNUAL #6 --AnnN.

THAT GAILY CAPARISONED ADVENTURER IS PUTTING UP AN ADMIRABLE STRUGGLE, MILADY, AGAINST CONSIDERABLE ODDS.

MY DARLING EROS, I THOUGHT YOUR CREDO WAS TO MAKE LOVE, NOT WAR.

EVERY RULE NEEDS ITS EXCEPTION, DEAR JANET, AND THE WARRIOR'S COURAGE SHOULD EARN HIM A BETTER FATE THAN THE WIZARD'S DUNGEON.

EROS, THEY HAVE HIM!

< SO MUCH FOR MY BEING A NICE GUY. >

< I'M TRYING SO HARD NOT TO HURT THESE KIDS, I'M GETTING CLOBBERED. >

< AND NOW, WHEN I NEED THEM MOST, MY STRENGTH-- MY POWERS-- ARE DESERTING ME! >

18

IT IS AS THE MASTER PROMISED. KULAN GATH'S MAGIC -- CHANNELED THROUGH US-- HAS BROUGHT HIS HATED ENEMY LOW.

"KULAN GATH?!?" BUT THAT'S IMPOSSIBLE!

‹SO'S WHAT'S HAPPENED TO NEW YORK. IF THIS MEANS WHAT I THINK IT DOES, I'M IN BIG TROUBLE!›

HOLD! THE MASTER'S ORACLE, XAVIER, SPEAKS TO ME!

ANOTHER FOE IS CLOSE BY-- THERE, BY THE FIRE!

SHE'S JUST A GIRL. LEAVE HER ALONE.

HIS SHIELD MARKS HIM AS A CAPTAIN.

SO? STAND ASIDE, LOUT-- WE'RE ON THE WIZARD'S BUSINESS!

AND IF I REFUSE?

YOU AND YOUR COMPANIONS DEFY OUR DREAD LORD AT YOUR PERIL.

BRING ME THEIR HEADS!

A BRAWL -- THE PERFECT END TO A PERFECT EVENING, eh, SWEETHEART?!

ONLY IF WE WIN, NIGHTCRAWLER.

FOR SHAME, ROGUE -- TO HAVE SO LITTLE FAITH -- WHEN HAVE WE EVER LOST?

ALWAYS A FIRST TIME, SUGAR.

KTHOOM!

COLOSSUS AND SUNDER?!!

19

AS IS QUITE COMMON UNDER SUCH CIRCUMSTANCES...

...THINGS QUICKLY GET OUT OF HAND.

MEANWHILE...

THERE IT IS. OUR MOMENT OF TRUTH.

SCARED?

VERY.

MAKES TWO OF US.

YOU OKAY, YOU DON'T LOOK SO GOOD.

IT IS THE WOUND YOU GAVE ME-- BUT I CAN MANAGE.

IT IS A SHAME FATE CAST US AS RIVALS, CALLISTO.

BREAKS MY HEART, BLUE-EYES.

SHALL WE?

EMERGING A STEP LATER FROM THE BARRIER ARE A HARD-BITTEN MERCENARY WARRIOR...

...AND A SORCERESS-PRINCESS OF A HOUSE THAT WAS OLD BEFORE THE DAWN OF HISTORY, RESTORED TO PERFECT HEALTH BY SELENE'S ENCHANTMENT.

REGRETTABLY...

IN THE NAME OF KULAN GATH...

...SLAY THEM!!

AT ROUGHLY THE SAME MOMENT, BACK AT THE TAVERN...

REBEL SCUM, YOU ARE DOOMED!

THE LAD MAY HAVE A POINT, MY FRIEND. WE'RE CERTAINLY OUTNUMBERED.

MY TRIBE ALWAYS HAS BEEN, NIGHTCRAWLER, YET WE'VE NEVER BEEN BEATEN.

SO LONG AS WE LIVE, WE HAVE HOPE.

20

HOWEVER, ALL BUT FORGOTTEN IN THE MELEE, THE SCULLERY GIRL WHO WAS ITS CAUSE...

...REVEALS HER TRUE SELF.

THE SOULSWORD IS THE ULTIMATE EXPRESSION OF ILLYANA RASPUTIN'S POWER AS A SORCERESS. NO MAGICKAL ENTITY OR SPELL CAN WITHSTAND IT...

...AS HER ENSORCELLED BROTHER PETER DISCOVERS.

THE TOUCH OF HER ELDRITCH BLADE FREES HIM FROM KULAN GATH'S SLAVER SPELL.

BUT THE REACTION OF HIS COMRADES IS NO LESS SWIFT AND DEVASTATING...

...AS SUNSPOT SHATTERS THE FLOOR BENEATH HER.

ORDINARILY, ILLYANA WOULD SAVE HERSELF BY TELEPORTING TO LIMBO-- BUT THAT'S HER MUTANT POWER AND, THANKS TO KULAN GATH'S MASTER SPELL...

...SHE'S FORGOTTEN SHE POSSESSES IT.

SUDDENLY...

...THE ROOM ITSELF-- WALLS, FLOORS, CEILING, FURNITURE-- COMES ALIVE TO ENTOMB THE WARRIORS THREATENING ILLYANA AND THE BATTLING HEROES.

UNHAND HER!!

21

OUR COMRADES-- SLAIN TO A MAN!

ONLY SUNDER'S STRENGTH SHATTERED OUR PRISONS AND SAVED US.

WE HAVE THE MAN-SPIDER. THAT'S WHAT KULAN GATH WANTED MOST.

THESE OTHERS CAN WAIT!

THEY'RE GONE! VANISHED!! FLED!!!

YAY FOR US, WE WIN!

I OWE YOU MORE THAN I CAN EVER REPAY, LITTLE SNOWFLAKE -- MY LIFE, MY VERY SOUL!

PIOTR NIKOLIEVITCH--

WHAT ELSE WAS A SISTER TO DO?

WHO CAME TO OUR AID?! AND WHY?!!

SHE STRUCK WITH A MERCILESS BRUTALITY THAT MATCHED OUR FOES'!

I AM SELENE-- THESE, MY CHILDREN: AMARA and RACHEL.

AND I WAS FAR GENTLER THAN THEY WOULD HAVE BEEN WITH YOU, DEAR CAPTAIN, IN SIMILAR CIRCUMSTAN-CES. AT LEAST, THEIR END WAS QUICK AND RELATIVELY PAINLESS.

YOUR AGONIES AT KULAN GATH'S HANDS WOULD DEFY DESCRIP-TION.

I SAVED YOU FROM THAT. IN RETURN, I RE-QUIRE YOUR AID AGAINST THE FOUL SPECTRE WHO HAS SEIZED YOUR CITY.

AH, SELENE, WEREN'T YOU ALWAYS SAYING THAT OVER-CONFIDENCE...

Eh--?!?

22

... WOULD PROVE THE DEATH OF ME?!?

MISTRESS!?!

WHAT AN UN-EXPECTED PLEASURE-- TO MEET ONCE MORE SO HATED A FOE FROM THE OLD DAYS. AND REMOVE HER WITH SUCH CONSUMMATE EASE, YOUR PATHETIC REBELLION WILL PERISH WITH HER.

BUT I CAN-- AND WILL-- BE MERCIFUL TO THOSE CALLED MUTANTS. ABANDON YOUR SO-CALLED COMRADES WHO WOULD SOONER STAB YOU IN THE BACK THAN ACCEPT YOU INTO THEIR HEARTS AND HOMES. I OFFER THE WEALTH OF AGES, POWER, GLORY--ALL THE PLEASURES YOU CAN IMAGINE.

... IN RETURN FOR YOUR LOYAL SERVICE. DECIDE QUICKLY, MY FRIENDS. I SHALL NOT ASK AGAIN.

SORRY WE'RE LATE, SELENE. WHAT'S OUR NEXT MOVE ?!

MINUTES LATER...

KRONCH

ISHTAR'S GIRDLE !

DREAD ONE-- THE REBELS-- THEY'RE ...

GONE?!? WHERE?!?

I/CALIBAN DO NOT KNOW.

I / CALIBAN SEEK, BUT CANNOT FIND.

WHAT A PITY.

COULD IT BE, DEAR KULAN, THERE ARE LIMITATIONS TO YOUR ABILITIES? THAT YOU ARE, PER-HAPS, NOT QUITE SO OMNIPOTENT AS YOU LIKE TO THINK ?!

23

YOU WOULD DO WELL, SLATTERN, TO HOLD YOUR TONGUE, LEST I CARVE IT OUT.

AIEERRRGH!

TRUE, MY MASTER SPELL REQUIRES MUCH POWER AND CONCENTRATION. BUT THESE MUTANTS HAVE PROVEN UNCOMMONLY SUSCEPTIBLE TO MY WILL. I SHALL MOLD THEM INTO THE MOST FEARSOME WARRIORS ANY WORLD HAS EVER SEEN!

ALREADY, WITH THE MORLOCKS AND XAVIER'S NOVICE STUDENTS, YOU'VE SEEN THE FIRST FRUITS OF MY GENIUS.

SEARCH THE CITY, MY PROUD BUTCHERS-- FROM ITS TOP-MOST TOWER TO YOUR DARKEST MORLOCK CAVERN--

--I WANT THE REBELS IN CHAINS OR IN THEIR GRAVES BY SUNRISE!

YOU'RE POSITIVE WE'RE SAFE, CALLISTO?

NOWHERE'S "SAFE," FUZZY, WHERE A WIZARD'S CONCERNED. BUT I FIGURE THIS HOLE'S AS GOOD AS WE'LL EVER GET.

THE TUNNELS ARE ALL WARDED AGAINST THE SEEKER XAVIER'S POWER AND THIS IS ONE ONLY I KNOW ABOUT.

ORORO, I'M WORRIED ABOUT THE GIRLS. SELENE TOUCHED THEIR SOULS. SHE'S A PART OF THEM-- AS THEY ARE OF HER-- KULAN GATH COULD USE THAT BOND AGAINST US.

OR SELENE HERSELF COULD.

THE RISK MUST BE TAKEN, CALLISTO. WE NEED THEIR POWERS.

IF IT COMES TO A CHOICE, AMARA, WHICH SIDE--?

WE HAVE NO CHOICE, RACHEL, NOT REALLY. NOT ANYMORE. FIRST, LAST, ALWAYS, WE SERVE SELENE.

THE WIZARD'S GUARD IS DRAWN FROM YOUR TRIBE, CALLISTO, AND YOURS, ORORO. HE CALLED THEM MUTANTS.

IT IS SAID WE ARE TOUCHED-- OR CURSED-- AT BIRTH WITH MAGIC. FOR THAT "CRIME," MUTANTS ARE BRANDED OUTCASTS-- EVEN A LEPER IS MORE WELCOME THAN WE. BITTERNESS-- AND RAGE-- AT SUCH TREATMENT EXISTS IN ALL OUR HEARTS, NO MATTER HOW NOBLE OR INNOCENT.

SMALL WONDER KULAN GATH FINDS IT SO EASY TO TWIST US TO HIS FOUL SHAPING.

SELENE IS DEMON SORCERESS AND MUTANT BOTH.

AS AM I, GOOD CAPTAIN. KNOWING THAT, WOULD YOU DEFEND ME AS YOU DID BEFORE?

AMONG MY PEOPLE, YOUNGSTER-- FOR WHOM I AM NAMED-- A PERSON IS JUDGED BY DEEDS. EVERYONE IS CREATED EQUAL-- FREE IN BODY AND SPIRIT-- WITH THE SAME RIGHT TO LIFE, LIBERTY, AND THE PURSUIT OF HAPPINESS.

BUT I WARN YOU, SELENE AND KULAN GATH ARE TWO OF A KIND.

24

WE DON'T TRUST HER EITHER, CAP.

BUT WE NEED HER.

AS, I SUSPECT, SHE NOW DOES US. THE PARAMOUNT THREAT, HOWEVER, IS KULAN GATH. WHATEVER OUR SUSPICIONS OF SELENE, WE *KNOW* WHAT HE WILL DO-- ENSLAVE THE WORLD, CAPTAIN, INCLUDING YOUR PROUD AMERICA.

ONCE HE IS BEATEN, THEN WE CAN WORRY ABOUT HER.

ORORO, SHE MAY BE DEAD ALREADY-- OR WORSE.

WE'VE LOST OUR STRONGEST WEAPON, BEFORE THE BATTLE'S EVEN BEGUN.

THAT IS WHAT KULAN GATH NO DOUBT BELIEVES. SO WE SHALL TURN THAT BELIEF TO OUR ADVANTAGE.

CONFRONT RAW POWER WITH STEALTH AND TRICKERY, CONFOUND HIS SORCERY WITH OUR WITS. FOR ALL HIS BOASTING, NIGHTCRAWLER, HE IS NO GOD, MERELY A MAN.

WE MAY FAIL, BUT WE MUST TRY.

MY ENTIRE LIFE HAS BEEN A CRUSADE AGAINST EVIL, AGAINST THOSE WHO WOULD ENSLAVE THEIR FELLOW MAN.

THERE'S NO DOUBT IN MY MIND ORORO IS RIGHT. SOME OF US ARE MUTANTS, OTHERS AREN'T-- BUT THAT ISN'T IMPORTANT. IF WHO WE ARE AS *PEOPLE*-- IF WHAT WE BELIEVE IN-- IS TO MEAN ANYTHING...

...WE HAVE TO MAKE THIS STAND.

MY FRIENDS, IN THE NAME OF THOSE KULAN GATH HAS SLAIN AND MAY YET SLAY-- AND THE DREAMS HE'S TRAMPLED INTO NIGHTMARES-- LET THE WORD GO FORTH:

...*AVENGERS ASSEMBLE!*

NEXT: RAIDERS OF THE LOST TEMPLE!

A DAY AGO, THIS WAS THE PROUDEST CITY IN THE PROUDEST COUNTRY ON THE FACE OF THE GLOBE, A MODERN METROPOLIS BARRELING HEADLONG AND HELTER-SKELTER INTO THE 21st CENTURY.

THEN, A SPELL CAST BY THIS DEMON-SORCERER TURNED TIME BACK UPON ITSELF, RECREATING ON MANHATTAN ISLAND AN AGE UNDREAMED OF.

EVERYTHING-- LIVING AND UNLIVING-- WAS INSTANTLY TRANSFORMED. CARS BECAME HORSE DRAWN CHARIOTS; POLICE, CIVIC GUARDS; GUNS, SWORDS.

ANYONE PENETRATING THE MYSTIC BARRIER SURROUNDING THE ISLAND WAS-- AND IS-- SIMILARLY AFFECTED. AND ONCE WITHIN THAT WALL OF ENERGY, THEY LOSE ANY DESIRE TO LEAVE. TO THEM, THIS IS REALITY.

TO ENFORCE HIS RULE, KULAN GATH ENSLAVED THE MORLOCKS-- A BAND OF RENEGADE MUTANTS WHO LIVE IN CATACOMBS BENEATH THE UNSUSPECTING CITY...

...THEIR FEATURES AND GARB CHANGING TO REFLECT HIS COMPLETE DOMINATION.

IN ADDITION TO THE MORLOCKS, HIS VICTIMS INCLUDE THE NEW MUTANTS--

-- THE NOVICE STUDENTS OF CHARLES XAVIER, HIMSELF CRUELLY BOUND TO KULAN GATH'S SERVICE.

XAVIER IS THE GREATEST TELEPATH ON EARTH. IN HIS RIGHT MIND AND WORLD AND TIME, HE IS MORE THAN A MATCH FOR THE SORCERER.

BUT THE MASTER SPELL CAUGHT HIM BY SURPRISE -- IT WAS AN ATTACK AGAINST WHICH HE, AND HIS FELLOW HEROES, HAD NO TRUE DEFENSE.

IN ALL THE CITY, ONLY THESE FEW POSSESS THE FREEDOM AND ABILITIES TO CHALLENGE KULAN GATH. SOME ARE AVENGERS-- EARTH'S MIGHTIEST DEFENDERS-- LED BY CAPTAIN AMERICA.

THEIR COMPANIONS ARE MUTANTS. TO THEM, THE WIZARD HAS PROMISED UNTOLD RICHES, IF ONLY THEY WOULD JOIN HIM. A TEMPTING OFFER, CON-SIDERING THEY ARE AT BEST FEARED-- AT WORST, HATED AND HUNTED AND SOMETIMES SLAIN-- BY THEIR FELLOW MAN, SIMPLY BECAUSE THEY EXIST.

BUT THESE MUTANTS ARE THE X-MEN-- AND KULAN GATH IS THEIR SWORN ENEMY.

ONCE BEFORE, KULAN GATH APPEARED IN NEW YORK TO ATTEMPT HIS GRAND ENCHANTMENT-- ONLY TO BE HURLED BACK INTO THE MYSTIC ABYSS THAT WAS HIS ETERNAL PRISON BY THE AMAZING SPIDER-MAN. TONIGHT, THAT HERO PAYS THE PRICE FOR HIS COURAGE AND VICTORY.

2

THY STRUGGLES ARE IN VAIN. THY FANTASTIC STRENGTH AND POWERS WILL AVAIL THEE NAUGHT AGAINST MY MYSTIC CHAINS.

AND LOOK NOT FOR AID AMONGST THY COMRADES. THY CITY LIES UNDER MY ENCHANTMENT AND THOSE HEROES NOT YET BOUND TO MY SERVICE-- AS THESE NEW MUTANTS AND MORLOCKS ARE-- WILL AID THEE NOT, FOR ONLY THOU REMEMBERS THE WORLD AND LIVES THAT WERE.

WONDERFUL-- EVEN IF I BUST LOOSE, I'M THE ONLY PERSON IN MANHATTAN WHO SPEAKS ENGLISH. NO ONE'LL UNDERSTAND A WORD I SAY, I'LL PROBABLY APPEAR TO THEM AS SOME SORT OF DEMON.

I DIDN'T THINK IT'D BE POSSIBLE TO HURT SO MUCH-- AND KULAN GATH'S BARELY BEGUN.

GEE, KULEY, I FIGURED YOU WERE TOO BIG-HEARTED A GUY TO BEAR A GRUDGE.

THY BRAVADO DOES THEE CREDIT, MAN-SPIDER.

SPIDER-MAN-- GET THE NAME RIGHT, WILLYA?! SHEESH!

HAVE A CARE, BOY. THAT MAY WELL BE THY EPITATH.

THIS IS BUT THE FIRST STEP. SOON, I WILL HAVE POWER ENOUGH TO SPREAD MY MASTER SPELL ACROSS THE FACE OF THE WORLD-- TO REMAKE IT, AND ALL HUMANITY, IN MY IMAGE!

NO FOOLIN'? TELL ME, KULEY-- WHAT PROVIDES THE POWER?

WHY, BLOOD, OF COURSE--THE HOT FRESH LIFE ESSENCE OF INNOCENTS...

... AND HEROES!

IT DOES MY SOUL GOOD TO HEAR SUCH SCREAMS.

I TRUST, MY DARLING SELENE...

...THOU WILT SING AS SWEETLY...

HAD I MY MAGICKS, DOG...

BUT YOU DO NOT. MY SPELLS HAVE RENDERED YOU--

--AND THE ENCHANTER, STEPHEN STRANGE-- QUITE HELPLESS.

TSK, TSK, TSK-- HAVE MY GUARDS USED THEE UNKINDLY, WENCH? FOR SHAME!

THOU WERT MY GREATEST FOE.

THOU DESERVE GENTLER TREATMENT.

THERE, MUCH BETTER.

WENCHES ARE BETTER SEEN BUT NOT HEARD.

FOR ALL THY KNOWLEDGE OF THE ARTS ARCANE, THOU NOW HAST NEITHER MOUTH TO CRY ENCHANTMENTS...

...NOR HANDS TO DRAW THE SACRED SIGILS.

THOU ART WHAT SUITS THEE BEST, A CREATURE OF WANTON FLESH WHO EXISTS SOLELY TO BRING ME PLEASURE.

I CAN SEE IN THINE EYES HOW HAPPY THAT DOTH MAKE THEE.

SUNDER, MOONSTAR-- WOULDST ALSO MAKE THY MASTER GLAD?

WE LIVE TO SERVE, DREAD ONE.

PRECISELY.

WHERE ARE THE OTHER REBELS?

WE DO NOT KNOW, LORD. TH... ESCAPED US.

4

A PITY.

I HAVE A LOW TOLERANCE FOR FAILURE, MY PETS.

BETTER BY FAR FOR THOU TO PERISH IN BATTLE THAN RETURN IN DEFEAT AND DISGRACE TO FACE MY WRATH. I SHALL NOT BE SO GENTLE-- OR FORGIVING-- A SECOND TIME.

XAVIER, COME FORTH! WHERE ARE MY ENEMIES?!

I / CALIBAN HEAR, MIGHTY ONE...

...BUT YOUR FOES REMAIN HIDDEN FROM THE SIGHT OF MY MIND'S-EYE.

THERE IS BUT ONE PLACE, LORD...

...WHERE YOUR SERVANT'S SCRYING POWER CANNOT SEE-- THE MORLOCK CATACOMBS! THAT MUST BE WHERE THE REBELS HAVE FLED.

" SPLENDID, SUNDER. I WANT THEM IN CHAINS BEFORE ME BY DAWN. OR, DEAR CHILDREN, THEIR FATE SHALL MOST ASSUREDLY BE THINE. "

UPTOWN, IN WHAT ONCE UPON A TIME...

...HAD BEEN THE NEW YORK PUBLIC LIBRARY...

A GUTTED RUIN-- THERE IS NOTHING LEFT !

5

WASP, SEARCH THE TEMPLE FOR ANY SURVIVORS.

THE REST OF YOU, STAY ALERT! WHOEVER DID THIS MAY STILL BE AROUND!

AH HOPE YOUR LI'L LADY'LL BE OKAY, STARFOX.

YOU'LL FIND, ROGUE, THAT DESPITE HER DIMINUTIVE SIZE, JANET CAN TAKE GOOD CARE OF HERSELF.

EROS--STARFOX!!

WASP! BY THE SACRED RINGS, WHAT AILS YOU, LASS?!

HORRIBLE--THE PRIESTESSES-- BUTCHERED, THEIR BODIES-- oh, IT WAS AWFUL!

MY HOPE WAS THEY MIGHT PROVIDE...

...WEAPONS--KNOWLEDGE TO USE AGAINST KULAN GATH. I FEAR, CAPTAIN, THE SORCERER HAD A SIMILAR NOTION.

DON'T DESPAIR, ORORO--

--LOOK OUT! NIGHTCRAWLER-- SNIPER ON THE WALL!

ON MY WAY, MY FRIEND!

BLANG.

A PRETTY PRIZE, THIS-- ANYONE KNOW HER?

I AM ARILYNN, YOU TELEPORTING DEVIL, CHIEF ARCHIVIST OF THE TEMPLE!

DO WITH ME WHAT YOU WILL, DOGS, MITRA SHRIVEL YOUR SOULS!

WE MEAN NO HARM, LADY.

YOUR HANDI- WORK SAYS OTHER- WISE.

THIS MASSACRE WAS NOT OUR DOING.

LIAR!

HOW CAN YOU SAY THAT WHEN AMONGST YOU STANDS CALLISTO, COMMANDER OF THE WIZARD'S OWN GUARD?!

6

BEFORE ORORO CAN REPLY...

IN THE NAME OF *KULAN GATH,* YIELD, TRAITORS--

--OR *DIE!*

THAT SCARLET WITCH HAS IMPRISONED MY BROTHER IN THE CRIMSON BANDS OF *CYTTORAK!*

BUT NOT FOR LONG *!*

ILLYANA RASPUTIN IS A DEMON SORCERESS IN HER OWN RIGHT AND HER *SOULSWORD* IS THE ULTIMATE EXPRESSION OF THAT POWER.

NEITHER ENCHANTMENTS NOR MAGICKAL BEINGS CAN WITHSTAND IT.

THERE ARE WARRIORS ALL OVER THE PLACE--

--TOO MANY TO FIGHT--

--FALL BACK TO THE CATACOMBS!

UNFORTUNATELY...

FOOLISH CALLISTO, DID YOU THINK OUR MASTER SO CARELESS AS TO LEAVE YOU A MEANS OF ESCAPE?!

THIS CREATURE, THE *VISION,* IS ANIMATE EARTH AND STONE, AS IMPERVIOUS TO HARM AS MY OWN BODY OF LIVING STEEL.

OF US ALL, ONLY THE STRENGTH OF *COLOSSUS* IS HIS EQUAL.

IT FALLS TO ME, THEN, TO PROTECT MY COMRADES.

YOWZA, *YOWZA*, *YOWZA*-- COME ONE, COME ALL!

TAKE YOUR BEST SHOTS, SUCKERS, THEY'RE *NOTHIN'* T' ME!

OUR BLADES SHATTER AGAINST *ROGUE'S* CRYSTAL HIDE!

CANNONBALL -- YOU'RE NEEDED, LAD!

MAH PLEASURE, GREYBEARD!

WHAMMO!

I HAVE THE WENCH--

-- BY THE *UNHOLY!?!* MY BODY-- TURNING TO *CRYST--*

NO! AH'VE ABSORBED HIS HUMANITY, MY GEMFORM'S BECOME FLESH AN' BLOOD--

NOW ISN'T THAT A CRYING SHAME!

ROGUE?!?

8

ROGUE!

ORORO'S GONE BERSERK-- THE GIRL'S DEATH HAS DRIVEN HER MAD!

BLESS HER, SHE'S GIVING US THE OPPORTUNITY WE NEED. RACHEL, USE YOUR MINDBLASTS TO PUNCH A HOLE THROUGH THAT OUTSIDE WALL!

AS SOON AS SHE DOES, ILLYANA...

...CAST A CLOAKING SPELL TO HIDE US!

CAPTAIN AMERICA, WHAT OF ORORO?!!

SKRAM!

GO, MY FRIENDS, WHILE YOU HAVE THE CHANCE!

I SHALL HOLD THESE CURS AT BAY AS LONG AS I AM ABLE!

(SELF NEVER DREAMED ORORO POSSESSED SUCH FEROCITY.)

(SHE EVER SEEMED THE GENTLEST OF CREATURES.)

(HER EFFORT IS MAGNIFICENT-- WISH SELF POSSESSED SUCH COURAGE-- BUT THE ODDS ARE TOO GREAT. SHE IS DOOMED...)

(...UNLESS SELF RESCUES HER!)

≋GASP!≋

(RAHNE-- SHE GRABBED SELF, IS TRYING TO DO SELF INJURY!)

9

WHAT MANNER OF HORROR *ARE* YOU?!

LATER...

COAST IS CLEAR.

I TRUST, ARCHIVIST, YOU BELIEVE US NOW.

SAVE YOUR RAGE, CALLISTO, FOR THE ONE WHO TRULY DESERVES IT.

WHO'S HERE?

ROGUE IS DEAD, MY FRIEND, AND PROBABLY ORORO WITH HER.

STARFOX AND HIS LADY, I SAW CAPTURED.

‹ORORO, SELF IS FRIEND-- *WARLOCK!*›

‹NULL COMPREHENSION, ORORO'S SPEECH-- HOW WILL SELF COMMUNICATE, HOW WILL SELF EXPLAIN-- THAT CRY?!!›

‹EXHAUST BLAST-- SELF BECAME TOO HOT FOR RAHNE TO HOLD!›

SOME HELP *YOU* WERE, AMARA!

YOU HAVE POWER OVER THE EARTH ITSELF-- YOU CAN CREATE 'QUAKES, EVEN VOLCANOES-- WHY DIDN'T YOU *USE* IT?!!

I'M SORRY, ILLYANA-- I WANTED TO HELP, BUT I... I...

...COULDN'T!

‹MAKER FORGIVE SELF-- SELF HAS TERMINATED SELF'S BEST FRIEND!›

I WAS SO S-S-*SCARED!*

SEE WHAT YOU'VE DONE, SISTER. FOR SHAME!

DO NOT WEEP, LITTLE PRINCESS. WE WILL KEEP YOU SAFE.

ILLYANA SPEAKS LIKE SHE KNOWS THE GIRL-- AND EXPECTED BETTER OF HER. AMARA'S SOUL-BOUND TO THE SORCERESS *SELENE*-- AS IS YOUNG *RACHEL*--

--COULD THAT HAVE SOMETHING TO DO WITH IT?

CALLISTO, WHERE'S THE NEAREST ENTRANCE TO YOUR CATACOMBS? *CALLISTO?!*

NEXT STREET OVER.

SORRY. I WAS WONDERING WHAT WAS HAPPENING TO ORORO AND THE OTHERS.

MOONSTAR...

SAM?! CANNONBALL SLAIN, MY DARLING RAHNE DYING --

-- BY THE ACCURSED, REBELS, YOU'LL *PAY* FOR THEIR LIVES!

FROM EACH OF THE PRISONERS, DANIELLE MOONSTAR MANIFESTS REAL-AS-LIFE PSYCHIC IMAGES...

... OF THE THINGS THEY FEAR MOST.

FOR EROS, IT IS BECOMING LIKE HIS *MAD BROTHER THANOS* -- WOULD-BE DESTROYER OF THE UNIVERSE.

FOR JANET VAN DYNE, IT IS BECOMING A WASP IN FACT AS WELL AS IN NAME.

PEACE, MOONSTAR.

MASTER, I CLAIM THEIR LIVES --!

AND I SAY THEE, *NAY.* I HAVE OTHER PLANS FOR OUR PRISONERS. WHEN I AM DONE, THEN YOU MAY HAVE THEM.

MOURN NOT FOR THY WEREWOLF, MY POWER ALREADY RESTORES HER...

... EVEN AS IT RESHAPES THESE REBELS MORE TO MY LIKING.

THE MAN POSSESSES SUCH BEAUTY THAT NO LIVING BEING CAN RESIST HIM OR DO HIM HARM, WHILE THE WASP NOW DRINKS LIVES AND SOULS TO MAKE ME STRONG.

THOU HAST DONE WELL, MY PETS, BUT I WILL NOT BE CONTENT TILL ALL SELENE'S REBELS ARE BEFORE ME IN CHAINS...

... OR IN THEIR GRAVES.

Meanwhile...

< SPEECH IS USELESS, AND ORORO SEEMS NOT TO RECOGNIZE THE IMAGES SELF MANIFESTS OF HER TRUE SELF AS LEADER OF THE X-MEN. >

< WHAT NEXT?! HOW CAN SELF MAKE HER UNDERSTAND?!! >

THE DEMON HAS NOT HARMED ME -- INDEED, HIS GENTLE MANNER BELIES HIS FEARSOME MIEN. BUT WHAT THEN DOES HE DESIRE-- BLESSED GODDESS!?!

< MOTHER! >

I SEE HIM-- AND THE STRANGE FACES HE FORMS OF ME... AND NOW... ONE OTHER!

SHE IS A SPIRIT-- THE DEMON SEEMS UNAWARE OF HER-- SPEAKING TO MY SOUL. I... I KNOW HER!

THIS IS MADNESS-- I SPOKE AND THINK IN THE DEMON'S GIBBERISH!

THERE ARE PICTURES IN MY BRAIN-- THE DEMON, WARLOCK, IS IN THEM, WE ARE COMRADES! HAS HE ENSORCELED ME?! HOW CAN SUCH THINGS BE MEMORIES?!!

YET-- I SENSE THEY ARE.

" THE CITY-- I SEE ANOTHER, COVERING IT LIKE A GHOST!

" EVEN AS I LOOK, THE DREAMSHAPES FADE-- AS DO THE STRANGE WORDS AND MEMORIES-- I AM MYSELF AGAIN. EXCEPT I KNOW NOW...

"...THAT SELF IS A LIE. "

Elsewhere...

SO YOU'VE HEARD OF HIM, LADY ARILYNN?

AN ARCHIVIST'S PASSION, CAPTAIN AMERICA, IS TO LEARN. ABOUT EVERYTHING AND EVERYONE.

KULAN GATH WAS AN APPRENTICE TO THE LORD OF THE BLACK RING, THE ARCHMAGE THOTH-AMON. BUT HE WAS FORCED TO FLEE STYGIA AFTER BEING CAUGHT PRACTICING MAGICKS THAT EVEN THE SONS OF SET CONSIDERED ABOMINABLE.

HE WANDERED THE WORLD, BECOMING A WIZARD OF AWESOME, INCALCULABLE POWER. IT IS SAID THERE ARE FEW, IF ANY, THAT ARE HIS EQUAL.

12

BY RIGHTS, HE SHOULD HAVE CARVED HIMSELF AN EMPIRE-- HE OFTEN TRIED, BUT SUCCESS ALWAYS ELUDED HIM. FOR SUCH A BRILLIANT MAN...

...HE COULD, ON OCCASION PROVE HIMSELF INCREDIBLY STUPID.

A GOD WITH FEET OF CLAY-- BUT STILL A GOD, COMRADES, WHO COULD REDUCE US TO ASHES WITH A GESTURE.

HE HAS LIMITS, NIGHT-CRAWLER.

OUR CONTINUED FREEDOM IS PROOF OF THAT. AND WE'RE NOT WITHOUT MAGICKAL RESOUR-CES OURSELVES.

ILLYANA EVENS THE ODDS SOME-WHAT, AND ONCE WE FREE SELENE...

ASSUMING SHE'S STILL ALIVE, HOW DO YOU PROPOSE WE GET INTO THE PALACE TO RESCUE HER?

THE OLD FASHIONED WAY, ELF...

"... THROUGH THE FRONT DOOR. "

YAWWWWWN!

HALT! WHO GOES THERE?!

IT'S AWFULLY LATE, WHY WAKE HIM?

PRISONERS FOR OUR DREAD LORD.

WAIT HERE, WHILE WE SUMMON THE CAPTAIN OF THE GUARD.

IT'S AWFULLY LATE, WHY WAKE HIM?

DO IT IN THE MORNING.

WE'LL DO IT IN THE MORNING.

LET US PASS.

YOU CAN PASS.

THAT WAS EASY! MY MINDSPELL WILL ENSURE THEY REMEM-BER NOTHING, CAP. I ALSO "HEAR" ECHOES OF SELENE'S THOUGHTS!

GREAT WORK, RACHEL-- LEAD THE WAY!

3

HOWEVER, AS OUR HEROES DISAPPEAR INTO THE SHADOWED, SILENT CITADEL...

DEAR, FOOLISH BOYS, OUR LORD AND MASTER EXPECTS BETTER OF THOSE WHO SERVE HIM. YOU WERE TAKEN BY SURPRISE AND DECEIVED *FAR* TOO EASILY.

IT IS HIS HOPE YOUR COMRADES...

...WILL PROFIT FROM THIS EXAMPLE.

AT ROUGHLY THE SAME MOMENT...

THIS PASSAGE SHOULD TAKE US DIRECTLY BENEATH KULAN GATH'S PALACE.

YOU KNOW OUR TUNNELS ALMOST AS WELL AS I, ARILYNN.

THAT'S PRAISE INDEED, CALLISTO.

I'VE ALREADY TRIED TO DISCOVER EVERYTHING I COULD ABOUT THE CITY AND ITS PEOPLE--JUST NATURALLY NOSY, I GUESS.

THE WOMAN HAS COURAGE. IN SPITE OF MYSELF, I LIKE HER.

BUT THE MORLOCKS' SALVATION HAS BEEN THE FACT THAT OUR LAIRS ARE *SECRET.* ANYONE-- ESPECIALLY A HUMAN-- WHO UNCOVERS THEM THREATENS OUR VERY SURVIVAL...

...AND MUST BE *DESTROYED.*

SURPRISE, CAL! KULAN GATH ANTICIPATED YOUR VISIT. HE ASKED US TO PROVIDE A PROPER RECEPTION.

SUNDER!

IT'S AN *AMBUSH!!*

14

WITH BUT A BLOW, REBEL, I CAN SMASH YOU TO A PULP!

ONLY IF YOU CONNECT, SUNSPOT!

ON THE OTHER HAND...

...YOUNG PRINCE...

BAMF

...SOLELY FROM SUNLIGHT...

...THE STRAIN IMPOSED BY MY MULTIPLE TELEPORTS...

...SINCE YOUR POWER DERIVES...

BAMF

BAMF

... SHOULD SPEEDILY DRAIN IT AND REVERT YOU TO HUMAN.

MY SOULSWORD CAN FREE MY FRIENDS FROM THE SLAVER SPELL, BUT RAHNE GRABBED ME--

-- I CAN'T REACH HER WITH MY BLADE!

ELDRITCH ARMOR PROTECTS MY LEFT ARM-- BUT MY RIGHT ONE'S... BREAKING!

SUNDER-- TEAR THE TRAITOR LIMB FROM LIMB...

...WHILE I CONFRONT HER WITH SPIRIT-FORMS OF WHAT SHE FEARS AND HATES MOST...

... THE WOMAN SHE ONCE WAS, THE LIFE THAT SHE MIGHT HAVE BEEN!

NO, CURSE YOU, BRAT--

--NO!

I MAY HAVE NO FANTASTIC POWERS OR MAGICKS LIKE THE OTHERS-- BUT THAT DOESN'T MEAN I'M HELPLESS!

BRAVE WORDS AND A MAD ACT-- BELIED BY THE TERROR IN ARI-LYNN'S HEART--

-- BUT IF SHE DOES NOTHING, SHE KNOWS SHE'LL CURL UP IN A CORNER AND WAIT TO BE SLAUGHTERED.

15

THAT SHE WILL NOT DO. WHATEVER THE COST.

RRARRR!

THAT, RAHNE, IS ENOUGH OUT OF YOU! I'M IN YOUR DEBT, LADY ARILYNN.

YOUR TURN, CHIEF. AAIIEEEE!

AS DANI IS RELEASED FROM KULAN GATH'S CONTROL...

...SO, TOO, IS CALLISTO FROM DANI'S.

HER RESPONSE IS AS INSTINCTIVE...

...AS IT IS DEADLY.

BY THE TIME CALLISTO REALIZES WHAT SHE'S DONE, AND THAT ILLYANA COULD HAVE LIBERATED SUNDER AS SHE DID HER FELLOW NEW MUTANTS...

...IT'S TOO LATE.

SUNDER!

SLEEP WELL, DEAR FRIEND --YOU'LL BE AVENGED!

16

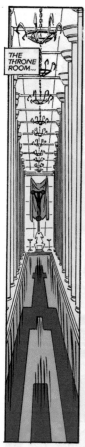

THE THRONE ROOM...

≥ GASP! ≤ THAT POOR MAN-- CAP, I FEEL HIS AGONY IN MY MIND, IT'S BEYOND BELIEF!

HELP HIM AS BEST YOU CAN, RACHEL, WHILE WE FIND SELENE.

THIS IS GOING FAR TOO EASILY, I DON'T LIKE IT.

CAP-- OTHER THOUGHTS-- THIS IS A TRAP!

GOOD GIRL-- USING YOUR OWN MAGICKS TO BLUNT THAT RED WITCH'S ATTACK!

THE ODDS ARE EQUAL, FRIENDS, WE CAN'T LET THEM STOP US.

AND SO, THE BATTLE IS JOINED-- WITH QUARTER NEITHER ASKED NOR GIVEN...

YOU'LL NOT ESCAPE THIS TIME, MUTANT!

YOUR ESSENCE, COLOSSUS, SO DELICIOUS-- LET WASPIE CLAIM IT FOR KULAN GATH!

HER TALONS-- CUTTING THROUGH MY STEEL SKIN-- DRAINING STRENGTH... MY VERY... LIFE!

17

AIEOWW!

SHOK!

UNHAND HIM, DEVIL!

TH-THANK YOU, CAPTAIN.

ORDINARILY, CAP'S SHIELD WOULD RETURN TO HIS GRASP...

...BUT, IN MID-FLIGHT...

A MOST AMUSING TOY, CAPTAIN.

COULD I HURL IT AS FAR AS THEE-- SAY...

...THROUGH THY HEART?!

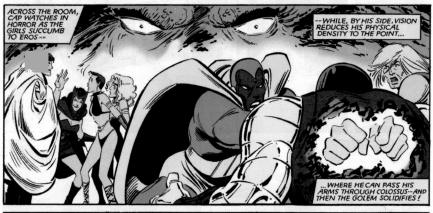

ACROSS THE ROOM, CAP WATCHES IN HORROR AS THE GIRLS SUCCUMB TO EROS--

--WHILE, BY HIS SIDE, VISION REDUCES HIS PHYSICAL DENSITY TO THE POINT...

...WHERE HE CAN PASS HIS ARMS THROUGH COLOSSUS--AND THEN THE GOLEM SOLIDIFIES!

THE TERRIBLE STRAIN IS TRAGICALLY MORE THAN EITHER CAN BEAR.

18

STEEL AND STONE SHRAPNEL SPRAY THE ROOM-- AND CAP'S MAIL SHIRT PROVES LITTLE PROTECTION...

...AS HE DROPS, STUNNED AND BLOODY, SURPRISED TO FIND HIMSELF STILL ALIVE.

< COLOSSUS -- VISION -- CAP-- EVEN THOUGH KULAN GATH MADE THEM DIFFERENT PEOPLE-- >

< -- THEY'RE STILL MY FRIENDS! I CAN'T JUST STAND BY... >

< ...AND WATCH THEM ALL BE MASSACRED! >

FOR A MOMENT, SPIDEY FEELS A SURGE OF HOPE...

...AS CALLISTO'S BAND BURSTS INTO THE THRONE ROOM.

BUT THEN, THE WIZARD-- HIS POWER HAVING TRANSFORMED THE MUTANT SCARLET WITCH INTO A TRUE SORCERESS--

-- USES HER SPELLS TO TURN THEM TO LIVING STATUES.

< NO MORE-- >

< -- NO MORE!! >

THE PAIN HE FEELS IS BEYOND BELIEF, YET NOT FOR AN INSTANT DOES SPIDER-MAN WAVER.

19

FLESH TEARS-- BUT THE CROSS BREAKS!

< THE AMULET! >

< HIS POWER RESIDES IN THE AMULET AROUND HIS NECK-- GET IT OFF HIM AND HE'S BEATEN! >

<A SUPREME EFFORT, BOY-- SUPREMELY WASTED. HAST THOU FORGOTTEN--

<--NONE BUT THEE CAN COMPREHEND THY BARBARIC TONGUE. >

< I AM AMUSED BY THEE NO LONGER, MAN-SPIDER. >

< THE TIME HAS COME TO DIE. >

HIGH ABOVE, HIDDEN IN RAFTERS BENEATH THE VENTILATION APERTURES THROUGH WHICH THEY SLIPPED UNDETECTED INTO THE PALACE...

< SELF UNDERSTANDS, EVIL ONE. >

< IF SELF HAS ONLY DECIPHERED ENOUGH OF ORORO'S LANGUAGE TO ENABLE SELF TO EXPLAIN... >

KULAN GATH'S NECKLACE IS IMPORTANT TO HIM?

AND WE ARE TO TAKE IT FROM HIM?!

WHY NOT, MY FRIEND! WE HAVE NAUGHT TO LOSE BY TRYING -- SAVE OUR LIVES AND OUR IMMORTAL SOULS.

20

[188]

BUT I NO LONGER POSSESS MY WIND-RIDING POWERS-- I CANNOT FLY-- HOW CAN I REACH HIM?

OH!?!

TRANSFORMING HIMSELF INTO A SET OF JET-POWERED WINGS, THE YOUNG ALIEN SCOOPS ORORO UP...

...AND DIVES FOR THEIR UNSUSPECTING FOE.

WHILE WARLOCK IMMOBILIZES THE WIZARD...

...ORORO GRABS HIS AMULET!

BUT THEN...

...WITH VICTORY LITERALLY IN THEIR GRASP...

SOMETHING'S SNATCHING THE NECKLACE AWAY--!

MANY THANKS, ORORO, FOR FULFILLING MY FAITH IN YOU--

--AND MY DESTINY!

SIMULTANEOUSLY, ON THE DAIS, SELENE BECOMES A WOMAN OF LIVING FLAME AND AT HER MENTAL COMMAND...

21

...A VOLCANO ERUPTS BENEATH WARLOCK AND KULAN GATH, CONSUMING THEM BOTH.

HA HA HA HA HA HA HA HA

KULAN GATH--YOU UTTER, COMPLETE, PATHETIC *FOOL*-- TO THINK ONE WHO KNEW YOU SO WELL WOULD ALLOW HERSELF TO BE TAKEN CAPTIVE WITH SUCH CHILDISH EASE.

THE GIRL, AMARA-- SHE WAS THE SORCERESS ALL ALONG!

I KNEW-- I WANTED TO TELL-- BUT SELENE'S SPELLS KEPT ME SILENT!

I'M TRYING TO RESIST-- TO REBEL-- BUT I CAN'T!

WHY RISK MYSELF, AFTER ALL, WHEN THERE ARE SO MANY NOBLE HEROES TO FIGHT-- AND DIE-- FOR ME?

NOW, *NONE* ARE LEFT TO OPPOSE ME AS I CAST THE *MASTER SPELL* OVER THE ENTIRE WORLD-- A WORLD SELENE SHALL RULE *FOREVER!*

PROGRESSIVE SYSTEMS COLLAPSE...

...LIFEGLOW QUICKLY FADING--

--BEYOND HOPE OF RESTORATION. BUT... ANOTHER WAY...

ORORO-- SELF CAN... MAKE YOU A BEING LIKE SELF-- YOUR LIFEGLOW STRONG, VITAL, YOU CAN *ACT!* SELF DOOMED-- WORLD MAY YET BE SAVED.

MUST WARN, THOUGH-- PROCESS... IRREVERSIBLE-- ONCE TRANSFORMED, NEVER AGAIN CAN... YOU BECOME ...HUMAN.

THERE ARE WORSE FATES.

22

SHE IS A CHILD OF NATURE, BUT WARLOCK'S TOUCH TURNS FLESH TO LIVING CIRCUITRY, BLOOD TO RAW ENERGY, A HUMAN BEING TO TECHNO-ORGANIC.

⟨WORLDSHIFT-- SELFCHANGE-- PROGRESSIVE TRANSMUTATION, SYSTEMS FLUXING, UNSTABLE-- SOUL- CORE SCREAM!⟩

⟨THOUGHTS RACING OUT OF CONTROL. PERCEPTIONS MAD WILD STRANGE...⟩

⟨...IT IS...⟩

⟨...SELF IS--⟩

⟨--I AM--⟩

⟨--ALIEN!⟩

SHE WEEPS-- FOR HER SLAIN FRIEND, FOR THE ORORO THAT WAS AND NEVER WILL BE AGAIN--

--HER TEARS NOT TRUE TEARS AT ALL BUT FLICKERS OF LIGHT...

...AND LASHES OUT AT SELENE...

...REPLICATING THE PROCESS, WITH ONE CRUCIAL EXCEPTION...

...AS SHE ABSORBS THE ENERGY, THE "LIFEGLOW" FROM HER FOE...

...RENDERING SELENE TOTALLY INERT.

THE SLAVER SPELL PERISHED WITH KULAN GATH. WITH SELENE IN VIRTUALLY THE SAME STATE, HER ENCHANT- MENTS ARE LIKEWISE BROKEN, ENABLING ILLYANA TO FREE AND RESTORE Dr. STRANGE.

MERCIFUL VISHANTI--!

ORORO??

GREETINGS, MAGE. MY ASSUMPTION OF WARLOCK'S FORM HAS RESTORED MEMORIES OF MY TRUE IDENTITY AND THE WORLD.

THOUGH A CAPTIVE, ORORO, I WAS AWARE OF WHAT TRANSPIRED.

MY PRAYER WAS THAT THE WIZARDS' DEATHS WOULD FREE THE CITY-- BUT THAT HAS NOT HAPPENED!

23

NO-- THINGS HAVE GONE TOO FAR. THE SPELL HAS ACQUIRED A LIFE OF ITS OWN. IF NOT STOPPED NOW, IT NEVER WILL BE.

EVEN I, THE MASTER OF THE MYSTIC ARTS, LACK THE POWER TO COUNTER IT DIRECTLY.

HOWEVER, THERE MAY BE AN ALTERNATIVE--ALTHOUGH, IN ITS OWN WAY, THE CONSEQUENCES COULD BE AS DEVASTATING. I SENSE IN MS. RASPUTIN AN EXTRAORDINARY ABILITY TO MANIPULATE THE FORCES OF TIME ITSELF-- IF I CAN WORK MY MAGICKS IN CONCERT WITH HER OWN, AND THIS OTHER, MUTANT TALENT...

IT IS DONE.

WELCOME, ALL, TO MY *SANCTUM SANCTORUM*.

THE FACT THAT WE STAND HERE UNTRANSFORMED MEANS WE SUCCEEDED.

WHAT YOU JUST EXPERIENCED WAS A *TEMPORALSPACIAL CLAUDICATION*-- IN ESSENCE, WE USED THE POWER OF THE VILLAINS' MASTER SPELL TO TURN TIME BACK UPON ITSELF, TO RETURN US ALL TO THE MOMENT BEFORE IT WAS ORIGINALLY CAST AND BY DOING SO, PREVENT IT.

WHAT STOPPED THE SPELL, DOCTOR, DO YOU KNOW?

NO, CAPTAIN AMERICA, I FEAR NOT. TWISTING THE TIMESTREAM AS WE HAVE DONE...

...INVOLVES DEALING WITH THE PRIMAL FORCES AND FABRIC OF THE UNIVERSE. WHO CAN SAY WHAT REPERCUSSIONS MIGHT RESULT?

WHAT OF THOSE SLAIN, MAGE...?

A PITY, IN SELENE'S CASE, AN EXCEPTION COULD NOT BE MADE.

NONE WERE, ORORO, FOR THIS NIGHT HAS YET TO EVEN OCCUR.

STEPHEN, ABOUT ILLYANA--?

THERE IS LITTLE I COULD TEACH HER OF THE ARTS ARCANE, CHARLES, AND SUCH KNOWLEDGE IS NOT WHAT SHE TRULY NEEDS--

--WHICH IS THE ENLIGHTENMENT AND GROWTH OF HER SPIRIT.

THAT CAN BETTER COME, NOT FROM A STRANGER, BUT THOSE WHO *LOVE* HER.

WILL ANYONE REMEMBER, DOCTOR?

HOW CAN THEY, MISS WILLIAMS, SINCE NOTHING HAPPENED?

ONLY WE IN THIS ROOM, WHO WERE AT THE NEXUS OF THE TIMESLIP, HAVE ANY AWARENESS OF WHAT MIGHT HAVE BEEN.

AS USUAL, THE *X-MEN* HELP SAVE HUMANITY-- AND NOBODY KNOWS IT. FOR ALL OUR HEROICS, WE MUTANTS ARE STILL OUTCASTS...NOTHING HAS CHANGED.

NOT QUITE, STORM.

I KNOW. AND FOR WHAT IT'S WORTH, I THANK YOU.

24

"I WONDER," ORORO MUSES SOFTLY, "WHAT THE CONSEQUENCES WILL BE OF OUR ACTIONS TONIGHT? HAVE WE, IN FACT, SAVED THE WORLD, OR MERELY DELIVERED IT -- AND US--

"-- TO A FAR MORE TERRIBLE FATE?"

...MUTANTS... INTEND TO SUPPLANT US "LOWER" CREATURES AS THE DOMINANT SPECIES ON THIS PLANET!

QUERY: LOCATION?

EARTH. NORTH AMERICA. MANHATTAN. TEMPORAL DATA ANOMALOUS-- THIS IS NOT WHERE I WAS, NOR WHERE I AM SUPPOSED TO BE!

IMMEDIATE SITUATION: CRIME IN PROGRESS, HUMAN LIFE THREATENED.

APPROPRIATE ACTION INITIATED.

WE... BELIEVE THE MUTANTS MENACE IS REAL--SQUAWRRK!

THE SHOCKBLAST SENDS JAIME RODRIGUEZ SPRAWLING...

... A CERTAIN NECKLACE FLYING FROM HIS JACKET...

...TO VANISH FROM SIGHT INTO THE MUCK AND OOZE.

AND IF A DAEMONIC VOICE SHRIEKS IN FUTILE PROTEST, NO ONE HEARS. NO ONE ANSWERS.

OBSERVATION: VICTIM ALIVE.

EASY, FELLA, YOU'LL BE OKAY.

WHAZZUP-- SOMEBODY... HIT ME.

DON'T WORRY, HE WON'T DO IT AGAIN.

OBSERVATION: ANTI-MUTANT SENTIMENT PREVALENT IN THIS SOCIETY.

CONCLUSION: IF MUTANTS EXIST, THEN, TRUE TO MY PRIME PROGRAMMING...

...NIMROD MUST SEEK THEM OUT... ...AND OBLITERATE THEM.

NEXT: FUN AND GAMES!

THAT'S ALL FOR NOW, MUTANT MANIACS! BUT WORRY NOT, AS THE UNCANNY X-MEN WILL RETURN IN THEIR NEXT ACTION-PACKED POCKETBOOK THE GIFT - COMING SOON!